A Rex-full Summer

A Thrifty Traveler's
Tribulations and Triumphs

Also by Helen (McCutchen) Buell Whitworth

The George McCutchen Family. A booklet of family pictures and stories. By Helen McCutchen Buell, published privately in Vancouver, WA, 2002. (Out of print.)

Betsy. An historical romantic novel circa 1850, based on McCutchen family history in Missouri. By Helen Buell, published by Trafford Publishing, 2005. A sequel is planned. Available on Amazon.com.

Riding a Rollercoaster with Lewy Body Dementia. A reference book for care staff and families. By Helen Whitworth, MS, BSN and James Whitworth, LBD Surviving Spouse, published by The Whitworths of Arizona, 2008. (Available only as a textbook.)

A Caregiver's Guide to Lewy Body Dementia. A reference book specifically for families and family caregivers. By Helen Buell Whitworth and James A. Whitworth, published by Demos Medical Publishing, 2010. Available in bookstores and online.

We are working on a book about early LBD which should come out in 2014.

All books (unless out of print) are also available on the
Whitworth website, LBDtools.com.

A Rex-full Summer

A Thrifty Traveler's Tribulations and Triumphs

Helen Buell Whitworth

Order this book online at www.trafford.com
or email orders@trafford.com

Most Trafford titles are also available at major online book retailers.

Printed in the United States of America.

ISBN: 978-1-4669-9699-1 (sc)
ISBN: 978-1-4669-9698-4 (e)

Trafford rev. 06/20/2013

Trafford
PUBLISHING® www.trafford.com

North America & international
toll-free: 1 888 232 4444 (USA & Canada)
phone: 250 383 6864 ♦ fax: 812 355 4082

This book is dedicated to my brother Bob, and his wife, Iris. They have been there for me all my life, through the joys and the sorrows, the fun and the work.

Acknowledgements

There are so many people who helped me to make this book what it is, but these are the ones who deserve a special vote of thanks: First there's my husband, Jim, who allows me to make loving fun of him, and who does so much to make it easier for me to just create. Then there's my writing group, who review every word and push me to write more and to publish what I might otherwise not. And finally, there are Ginger Fleishans, Peg Copas and Betty Olson, who find the mistakes and inconsistencies that I continually miss, even though I read it over and over.

Thank you, all of you.

Helen's Royal Flush

2. I Was Thrifty Before Thrifty was Cool

It was no surprise to those who know me that we chose a used vehicle, paid for in cash instead of a new RV with huge monthly payments. Long before it was politically correct to recycle containers, use up leftovers or buy second hand, I did all of this. It's not that I've ever been really poor—I simply like the challenge of being thrifty. Some might find this discouraging; I find it fun—most of the time.

My motto has been that it isn't only a new car that loses a large percentage of its value the minute it leaves the store. I love going to garage sales or thrift stores and finding something I want for a fraction of the price it would cost me elsewhere.

And so yes, I love a bargain, am very good at making do and prefer to buy secondhand. Jim is fairly frugal too, and although he has a typical male aversion to garage sales and thrift stores, he does appreciate my ability to find a bargain.

3. My Big Brother, My Mentor

I'm the one who really wanted Rex. I'd wanted a motorhome ever since my brother Bob and his wife Iris retired and started escaping cold Washington winters for the warmer climes of California. Over the years, they had a variety of rigs. My brother, a mechanic, would fix up each RV, and then they'd use it a year or two before they sold it and bought another. Now in their 80's, they still have a small motorhome they use for weekend trips nearer home.

I've always looked up to my brother, eighteen years my senior. Because he and Iris married before I was two, I've always thought of my brother and his wife as a unit—BobnIris. I guess I've tended to view them as mentors and to think that whatever BobnIris did was exciting. When they were parents of school-age children, they took their kids camping.

Years later, when I had school-age kids, we went camping. BobnIris square danced; I've square danced off and on for years. When they retired and became snowbirds, wintering in California and Arizona, I thought it sounded wonderful and knew that when I retired, that's what I'd want to do.

4. My Li'l Brother, My First RV

In the late 80's, I was widowed and living in Alaska. BobnIris had been traveling in their RV since the late 70's. Because I was still working, snowbirding for the whole winter wasn't an option, but I decided I could still get an RV. It would be a great way to get to know my state. You know, go camping in Denali, drive the Parks Highway to Fairbanks, go fishing on the spit in Homer, take the ferry to Kodiak . . . .

I wanted a vehicle small enough that I wasn't afraid to drive it, but large enough so that I and a companion could camp in it for several days. And of course, I wanted it to be inexpensive—both to buy and to operate. The second-hand 17-foot Toyota Chinook pop-top that I finally bought fit the bill perfectly with its low selling price and high miles per gallon.

The Toyota's license plate read "BRS212." The youngest of a large family, I'd always wanted little brothers. This in mind, I interpreted my license plate as "Brothers, aged 2 and 12" and named my camper "Li'l Brothers," which quickly became shortened to "Li'l Brother." I'd tell my co-workers that I was taking my Li'l Brother camping. When they commented that it was nice that I had family to go camping with me, I didn't correct them. After all, in those years, I had an active social life.

My Li'l Brother came with a major drawback. It had a stick shift and it had been years since I'd driven anything but an automatic. I had a friend drive it home and teach me how to shift. Once I got past the beginning jerks and jolts, I loved my Li'l Brother and drove him around Alaska for several years.

However, that was decades ago and I haven't driven a car with a clutch since then. We plan to tow Jim's 1999 five-speed Saturn. I've not been able to convince Jim that I can easily relearn to drive a stick shift. "The clutch is delicate," he hedges. I think it has something to do with the Li'l Brother having been mine to harm if I wanted to and the Saturn, his to protect.

I don't try too hard. It's only when I want to go somewhere alone that it's a bother, and then the hassle is more his than mine. He's the one who has to tag along when I go buy underwear or shop the thrift stores. And the bottom line: he has to drive both vehicles, Rex and the tow car, while I get to be the carefree passenger no matter which one we are in at the moment.

With my Li'l Brother, there was only me to do the driving. I had looked forward to camping, but unlike now, I didn't have a built-in companion to share the fun. I took my camper to a few out of town square dance festivals and went on a few camping trips around the state when I could find a friend to go with me. Mostly, it sat unused unless my car was in the shop and I needed wheels. I finally sold it and put my dream on hold, to be resurrected in the unlikely event that I remarried. I added "Can drive a motorhome" to my long "Perfect Man" list.

5. I Have A Driver

Several years after I retired and moved to Washington State, I did remarry.

I met Jim while vacationing in Arizona. Our first disagreement was about where we would live. Although Jim was born in Washington, he told me, "I left the rain and fog as soon as I could and I don't want to move back."

"After Alaska's snow and ice," I responded, "I find Washington's wet weather almost balmy and Arizona's summers, way too hot."

"That's what air conditioners are for."

"Air conditioners dry up my sinuses and bring out my allergies."

Last winter, I spent hours in an emergency room with a nosebleed. My body, used to damp climates, hadn't adjusted to the dry air.

"Well, Washington's humidity irritates MY sinuses." True. In a damp climate, Jim's nose turns into a leaky faucet. He has lost most of the feeling in his nose, which adds to the problem. Therefore, it has become my job as a caring spouse to let him know when his "faucet" is leaking.

We finally agreed to make our permanent home in Jim's roomy manufactured home in Arizona and summer in my small condo in Washington, reverse snowbirds—or sunbirds, as some call those of us who are escaping the sun instead of the snow. However, a couple of summers in my Washington condo showed us that what had been just right for me felt cramped for the two of us. I sold my condo, banked the money and began looking for just the right replacement.

That's when my dream of a motorhome stirred. A quiet, self-effacing man, Jim comes to life behind the wheel. He loves to drive, and in his youth, even raced cars. That worked for me. I happily rode shotgun and let him do the driving as we traipsed back and forth between Arizona and Washington.

I suggested that we could buy a motorhome with the condo money. "That way we'd have more mobility," I said. "Wouldn't it be great to travel in our own home?"

Jim wasn't interested. He'd been there, done that. In fact, he'd had several motorhomes and sold them all. "They aren't as much fun to drive as a smaller vehicle." I guess I had forgotten to add that to my list. You know, "WANTS to drive a motorhome."

"And besides," he added, "Gas is way higher now than it was in the 80's when I last had a motorhome." Well, that was surely true. In the fall of 2006, it was hitting an all time high of almost $2.00 a gallon.

The condo money sat in the bank for a year. Then I got another idea and my dream stirred again. Jim's first wife had died with a little known disorder called Lewy body dementia or LBD. He is still passionately interested in improving awareness about the disease, especially in the medical community. A retired nurse who loves to teach, I developed an educational program. When we began showing it to dementia care and assisted care facilities for free, we had lots of takers. My idea was to get the program accredited so we could charge for our time. Then, I told Jim, we could buy a motorhome, travel with it and do the programs.

Jim liked doing the program, liked educating people about LBD, but he was still lukewarm about committing to the responsibility of a motorhome. I did the math, showed him that our expenses, even in the unlikely event that gas should go as high as $3.00 a gallon, would be little different from the year round expenses of a summer home. He finally agreed. Oddly enough, even though he knew that we'd have less than half the space we had in the condo, space was never an issue. Apparently he finds a small space more acceptable when it is on wheels.

6. Just the Right One

With our limited funds—and our thrifty natures, we knew the motorhome would have to be a used vehicle. We called my brother, hoping to draw on his mechanical know-how and his past experiences with motorhomes.

Bob told us to be more concerned about the mileage than the age, and a few other tidbits. But, "I can't tell you much more without looking at the vehicles," he added. With him in Washington, a thousand miles away, we were on our own.

It took us months of looking to find Rex. Retired seniors on a short budget, we wanted to travel as inexpensively as possible. However, we rejected a lovely 21-foot Rialto travel van that got 20 miles to the gallon because it was too small and had only a four cylinder engine.

With a background in psychology and very little knowledge of mechanics, it has worked for me to "buy the seller" rather than the vehicle. However, we passed on a 30-foot Southwind whose owner exuded great pride in his vehicle. Jim thought the man's RV would fishtail in the wind and I didn't like the floor plan.

We wanted a used vehicle, but we rejected a roomy Holiday Rambler with all our basic requirements because it looked too well used. And so it went for months, one possibility after another. We'd begun to wonder if we'd ever find just the right RV. And then we saw Rex in that sales lot and we knew he was the one for us.

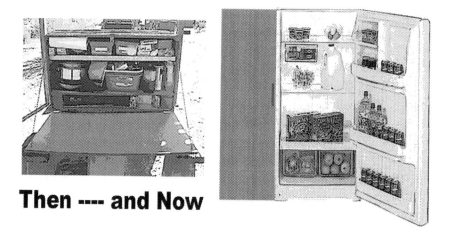

Then ---- and Now

7. Remembering Earlier Times

While Rex sits in his home behind the trash bins, we plan our shakedown cruise. Always alert for bargains, I've already signed up with a discount camping program called the Happy Camper. We decide on a three day outing to a RV park in Benson, a small community about 50 miles southeast of Tucson. My Happy Camper guide says it is a lovely campground—and with our HC discount, we can stay for half price. Way to go! I load up the inside of the RV while Jim loads up the RV basement compartments with tools and hoses and whatever else he thinks we'll need.

I carry my queen size bedding down Rex's hall and into the bedroom so I can make up the walk-around bed. I love that bed! What luxury! I remember my first camper. It was a 1962 International Scout, a boxy pre-SUV that Paul, my then-husband bought. He worked for the Forest Service and was into outdoorsy things like hunting and camping. When we moved to a wilderness area in Idaho and he said we'd have great fun exploring the area in the Scout. What went without saying was that he'd also have a sturdy hunting vehicle. Of course, the final selling point for me was that BobnIris took their kids camping. If they did it, it must be fun, right?

Imagine five people sleeping in a mini-SUV. Our son Ken got the front seat and a bunk bed setup took up the whole of the back of the Scout. Paul and I slept on the larger top level and the two girls slept on the floor underneath, in the narrower space between the wheel wells. I was younger then and more agile. Crawling in and out of cramped spaces was easier, but it was still a pain. Even so, I actually thought it was fun. I guess it helped that I was in great health, and that Paul and I were both thin and well under six feet tall.

Rex's queen-size walk-around bed made, I give it an appreciative pat. I'm no taller than I was then, but I'm certainly wider and I'm much less agile. Throw in the bathroom challenges that tend to come with age and yes, I love that bed! Jim likes it too, but not as much as I do. He is almost six feet tall and his feet hang over just a little—it's a short queen. I give the bed a final pat and move on to the kitchen.

This fancy kitchen with a side-by-side refrigerator-freezer, a four burner stove and plenty of storage space is a far cry from my Li'l Brother's tiny kitchenette. Of course, I'd thought it was wonderful compared to the portable kitchen box that Paul had crafted for the Scout. As I mindlessly fill Rex's kitchen cupboards with canned goods and store soft drinks in the shelves of the fridge door, I continue to reminisce.

Actually, I didn't always want to go camping, even with BobnIris setting an example. I avoided it years. I'd became soured on outdoor living when I was about ten and my parents and I spent a week tent camping on Long Beach, on the Washington coast. What I remember most about that trip, more than the squishy feeling of wet sand between my bare toes, more than the way the waves attacked me when I tried to swim in the ocean, was how my mother cooked potatoes on the camp stove—and morning after morning, burned them. For years, when anyone mentioned camping, visions of burned potatoes prompted a quick "Thanks, but no, thanks."

I smile as I close the refrigerator. No, I'm not sorry Paul talked me into getting the Scout. We had some fun times—and I never burned the potatoes. In fact, I seldom cooked potatoes. We were more the cold-cereal-and-sandwich type campers.

I'm ready to move on but the memories don't stop even though the next is one I'd just as soon forget. I see the Scout, irreparably wrecked, sitting in that awful ditch, where it had rolled because of my negligence. I wasn't trying to be careless. I knew it was important to leave a vehicle with a clutch either in gear or out of gear when you parked it on a hill. The problem was that I could never remember which and well, I simply chose wrong. It was the day before hunting season. "Anyone could have guessed wrong," I wailed to my husband as he reworked his hunting plans. He didn't respond with anything sympathetic. In fact, he wasn't speaking to me at all. Back in the present, I shrug and let it go. At least, because of that experience, I didn't have any trouble remembering to leave my Li'l Brother in gear when I parked it on a hill.

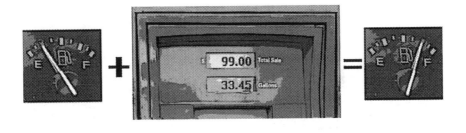

8. On The Road at Last

Our packing done, we excitedly pile into Rex and drive south towards Tucson and then Benson. Rex's 70 gallon gas tank is only a quarter full so we stop on our way out of town for gas. We expect it to cost a bundle and my stomach roils as I watch the dial spin. The numbers whiz past—$50, $75, and it's still going.

Finally it stops at $99. Jim presses the button again to add more gas, but nothing comes out. He frowns. But it's not full," he complains. The attendant comes over and explains that the pump stops automatically at $99 with credit cards. Jim will have to reinsert the card and start over to get more gas. He doesn't bother. I shake my head. It's hard to believe that we've put almost a hundred dollars of gas into that tank and it is only three quarters full. Of course, instead of the $2.50 a gallon that gas cost when we bought Rex, gas is now almost $3.00. I gulp. We are going to have to sell a lot of programs.

What a way to wake up!

9. A Bump in the Road

In a second hand unit, there are usually little foibles that at the time of sale seem unimportant. One of Rex's was that the fridge door latch had been broken and replaced with a plain handle. No, problem, we thought, because there was still a magnetic latch that worked just fine. Or it did until a lurching turn out of the gas station flings the door open and spills my carefully stored food on the floor. Worse, it damages the door's fragile aluminum hinges and completely breaks one. Perhaps if I hadn't put those cans of soda in the door . . . .

Jim re-hangs the door and props it shut with a spring loaded bar from a nearby hardware store. Although Jim later fixes the hinge, we know that the same thing could happen again so the bar becomes a fact of motorhome life. I easily duck under the, for me, eye-level bar. Since the bar hits Jim at neck level it takes only one near hanging to teach him to duck too.

We leave behind an urban skyline of palm trees and high rises and head out into the open desert punctuated by towers of saguaro cactus and bright green ocotillos. It's April and the desert is at its best. The ocotillos sport long spikes of brilliant orange flowers, the prickly pear show off with blossoms of pink and white and the saguaros wear crowns of waxy white blooms. Sitting high in the motorhome, we get a great view. We pass Maricopa, where for a while, new houses were going up every day. It was to be Phoenix's new bedroom community. However, the rising gas prices are making the 45 mile drive much more expensive. Whole rows of houses sit empty or half built—a ghost community, but it isn't anywhere near Halloween.

In Tucson, we look for a RV junk yard we'd heard about, a place where we hope to find a refrigerator door replacement. That's when I learn that my brother's statement that it was just as easy to drive a long vehicle as a short one isn't quite correct. Although driving on the highway may be, driving—and especially parking—on city streets is not. We find the yard, but no nearby Rex-sized large parking spaces, so we drive on by and head out of town. We will look for our door replacement in Phoenix—when we are driving a vehicle easier to park than Rex.

Jim spots a Camping World sign so we have to stop. "Why?" I ask. I'm eager to get to Benson and try out their swimming pool after a day of traveling.

Jim answers that he wants to check out prices for some items for Rex. Costco Wholesale stores are staples for Jim. When we are home, I tease him about needing a Costco fix every week, and when we travel, we have to stop at every one he sees. I now find that, when he's in motorhome mode, it's the same with Camping World.

10. Surprise Stop

Our Camping World shopping done, we leave Tucson. We zip contentedly along the desert highway toward the San Pedro Valley and Benson, with the sun sinking into the horizon. Life is good. The softly purring motor and the steady movement of our rig lulls me to sleep.

And then I awake with a jerk. We are slowing down and Jim is steering Rex over to the side of the road. "What's wrong? Why are you stopping?" I ask. We can't possibly be there yet.

"It's not me—it's the RV." Jim says as he manages to pull off the two lane highway onto a gravel shoulder just barely wide enough for our oversize vehicle. A big truck that was following us swooshes past. We sway wildly.

"The engine is running fine." Jim demonstrates by pressing down on the gas and making the engine roar. "But we aren't going anywhere." He's right. Even when the engine revved up, we didn't move an inch.

I realize I have another emergency. I had abdominal surgery several years ago, and since then, my bowels tend to react when I'm very scared. I need a bathroom—quickly. I leave Jim to deal with Rex while I run to use the bathroom, ever so thankful that we have one to use. There are some advantages to taking your home along with you when you travel, and this is definitely one of them.

That taken care of just in time, I go back up front. "So why . . . ?" I ask. He's the car person. He is supposed to know all this stuff. More cars pass, each one causing the RV—and me—to wobble. I'm still scared and grateful for our portable bathroom. If this keeps up I may need it again soon.

My husband shakes his head. "The power isn't getting to the wheels. Maybe it's the transmission." He presses on the gas again. The engine revs but we don't move. Jim turns off the motor and sits with his shoulders hunched and his head down. I relate. In fact, I feel like crying. What now? I suggest we call our new RV road service plan but Jim isn't ready to do that yet. "What if, when they got here, it works fine?" he asks.

Yeah, I think, what if. If that's what it takes to feel safe again, I'm willing to look a little stupid.

Jim, like any man who prides himself on knowing his mechanical stuff—even when he doesn't, isn't ready to cry "Uncle" yet. "Let's just wait a while and see what happens."

We wait, rocked by every passing vehicle. What if one of those trucks blasting by us gets a little too close and crashes into us? What if one of those wobbles turns into a roll over? What if . . . . ? Not a good line of thought. I make another dash for the bathroom.

After about twenty minutes and many passing cars and trucks, Jim tries again. He turns the key and shifts the automatic transmission into drive. The motor purrs. I hold my breath as he steps on the gas. Rex inches forward. Jim grins one of his huge grins—the kind that lights up his whole face—and heaves a great sigh. I shout "Hurrah!" Things are looking up.

"Maybe, it is just low on transmission oil," Jim suggests. He takes the first exit that will allow us to return to Tucson—and the Camping World store where we can get some transmission oil to hopefully, fix the problem.

Guliver "Rex" among the Giants

11. Gulliver among the Giants

It is truly dark now and we need to find a place to camp for the night. It's been a big day. I'm tired. More importantly, Jim is tired. Being the driver, he didn't get to nap. Since we hadn't seen any RV parks on the way out of Tucson, we look for a spot where we can dry camp. We find that spots where a 34-foot vehicle can stop along the road at night are scarce—non-existent, actually.

Then, pointing, I ask, "What are all those lights?"

"I'll bet that's an overnight truck stop," Jim answers. "Maybe we can stay there." As we draw closer, I see a brightly lit restaurant and gas station with several long rows of lights behind them. Yes, trucks, no doubt stopped for the night. "Sure, let's give it a try," I say. Jim pulls in and drives along between two rows of semis.

Until now, our motorhome has seemed huge as we looked down from our cab onto other vehicles on the road. In a twist of perspective, it has become a midget flanked by lines of giant trucks. Jim spots an opening on the left between two trucks and pulls in, turns off the motor and sits back with a happy sigh. We spend our first night in the new motorhome in a truck stop, with a background of running motors, but we are too tired to care.

In the morning, after a night of trying to sleep while listening to dozens of loud generators—apparently many truckers have loads that require 24-hour refrigeration—we head over to the restaurant to try out the trucker's food. I look back and gaze in amazement at three rows of trucks, rows that must stretch for a couple of city blocks. I run back to get my camera and take photos while truck drivers grin and watch the silly tourist.

Back in Tucson, we visit Camping World as planned. Jim finds the right kind of oil and pours it in. Then we hurry towards home. A couple of hours later, we drive Rex into his parking space behind the dumpsters, happy that he didn't balk again. Maybe the oil *was* the answer.

12. Rex is for "Tyrannosaurus Rex"

In the two months before we head north, we discover more problems. We find and fix a leak in the gas tank—a project which added almost a thousand dollars to Rex's price.

Then we discover that the dash air conditioning, which worked fine when we bought the RV, is no longer blowing cold air. Since fixing it will be even more expensive than the gas tank, we decide to wait and talk to Bob about it. "After all," we say, "the weather will be cooler once we leave Arizona."

"I've decided that "Rex," is really short for "tyrannosaurus rex," Jim comments. I think he is wishing we'd bought that 30-foot RV with the proud owner, even if it didn't have a tag axle.

Some of our expenses are planned. Because we will tow the Saturn, we need a tow bar, hitch assembly and brake lights. Together, these would have cost over a thousand dollars new, but, quintessential bargain hunter that I am, I have both *craigslist* and *eBay* bookmarked on my computer. I find the tow equipment on *craigslist* for half the price it would be new. Even so the cost of our motorhome is adding up and we haven't yet left Arizona.

Jim tells me that something called an inverter would allow us to run small appliances like our laptops without running the generator when we camp outside an RV park. Wonderful! I find one on *craigslist* for a very good price. It is delivered only days before we leave, so we put it aside to install when we get to BobnIris's.

In the meantime, gas hits $3.75. I'm beginning to wish we'd bought that little 21-foot Rialto travel van.

It is now late May and the temperature has already hit three digits. We want to escape the heat, but we are still concerned about the transmission. Nevertheless, we decide to cross our fingers, and as Jim says, "Make a run for it."

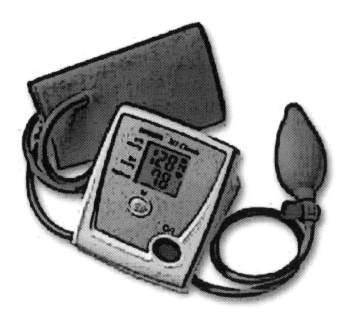

13. Cardiac Alert

Jim had a quadruple artery bypass a couple of years ago. Every six months he visits his cardiologist who has always told him he was doing fine. However, this time Dr. Beal is concerned. Jim's blood pressure is slightly too high. He increases Jim's medication and tells him, "I want you to keep a daily record of your blood pressure and make an appointment to come back in a week."

"We're planning to leave for the summer in a few days," Jim answers. "Should we postpone our trip?

"No, go ahead," Dr. Beal scribbles his email address on a prescription pad and hands it to Jim. "Just email me in a week with the readings." He thinks a moment, then, "If we still need to change your prescriptions, do you have a way to get them filled?"

Yes, like most snowbirds, we do. We get our medications at Costco, which has outlets nearly everywhere we plan to go. If Dr. Beal needs to prescribe another medication, he can call it into the Mesa Costco. And then we will go to the one nearest wherever we are camped and ask their pharmacy to have the prescription transferred.

It's leaving day when we remember that Jim hasn't picked up the extra medication Dr. Beal ordered. We take time out from loading Rex to go get it. There, we discover they only have enough in stock to fill half the prescription. "But," the clerk tells Jim, "You can pick up the rest of your prescription tomorrow."

"Tomorrow, we'll be gone," Jim counters. However, this half prescription will last until we get to BobnIris's in Everett.

"Just explain and ask the pharmacist there to transfer the other half," our Mesa clerk assures us.

That dealt with, we dash back home to finish loading up the RV.

14. Froggy

With Rex parked in front of our home, we pack out the final items for the trip. I've already transferred our program and sales information to my laptop. Now, we put both of our laptops into the RV, along with our other electronics: two cell phones and a computer phone, a brand new Wi-Fi printer, a projector and screen, two digital cameras and "Larry," our portable Lowrance brand GPS. With our clothes, and anything else we think we might need for the next four months packed away in Rex's various drawers and compartments, we are almost ready pull out.

But first we have to "hook up." This isn't some singles meeting—it's attaching the tow car ("*toad*" in RV lingo) to the RV. I anxiously stand and watch Jim back the Saturn out of the carport. Rex's rear sits so close to the driveway that I have visions of our trip starting with a collision. Thankfully, Jim's spatial skills are much better than mine. Soon he has the little car maneuvered into place behind Rex.

The tow equipment comes in two parts—some heavy bars and cables that live on Rex's behind like a folded up tail when he's not traveling and a bar that is now a permanent fixture just below the Saturn's front bumper. The "hookup" occurs when we attach these two parts. Already, we've developed a system. First, Jim unfolds Rex's tail and together, we fit the two bars like puzzle pieces to the bar on the car, then insert pins and locks to keep them in place. Then I attach the safety chains while Jim attaches the brake lights. They go on the lid of the trunk, big red "frog eyes" with wiring that travels through the trunk, the body of the car out hinge side of the front door, under the hood and finally along the tow bar to its own connection on Rex. Now when Jim applies Rex's brakes, the Saturn's red "frog eyes" light up as well.

"But these are Toad eyes," Jim says with a grin.

I groan. "No, no, the Saturn is too cute to be an ugly old toad. He's a little gold frog." Now it's Jim's turn to groan. I'm not sure he likes the idea of me calling his precious baby a frog. But it is too late; Froggy now obediently follows Rex everywhere he goes.

It is late in the day when we finish hooking up and drive out the gate of our 55+ community. Jim planned it that way. "It will give us a chance to see how Rex does. If he can climb the hill to the rest area, then we've probably solved the transmission problem." Jim explains. We'll travel only a couple of hours and stop less than 50 miles west of Phoenix.

We drive through Phoenix, and again we leave the urban scene behind and travel through desert. Soon we climb into the barren hills the separate Arizona from California. It's difficult to find beauty here. Summer is in full swing and everything is a medley of browns with no stately saguaros or colorful ocotillos to relieve the monotony.

Rex does fine. No balking. No problems. By the time we get to the top of the hill where the rest area is, it is almost dark. It's been a successful day. We enjoy a relaxed dinner in Rex, leftovers from when I cleaned out our fridge at home. Then we clear the table and play a few hands of cards. When Jim installs the inverter, we will be able to run our computers and the TV even when we don't have outside electricity.

Ah, yes! This is the way to travel.

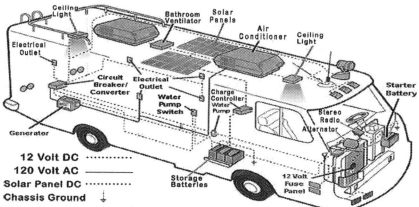

12 Volt DC ··············
120 Volt AC ──────
Solar Panel DC ··············
Chassis Ground ⏚

The typical RV has both 12-volt and 120-volt wiring circuitry. The power converter, batteries and solar panels supply 12-volt DC power. The 120-volt power is supplied by a generator and by electrical hook-ups in RV parks and campgrounds.

15. Power Primer

We are learning how important power in an RV is—and how different it is than in a home—or even in a smaller vehicle like my Lil Brother. Therefore, let me digress for a bit and share some of our hard-earned knowledge with you.

In line with our thrifty natures, Rex is set up for boondocking, or camping for free. That usually means dry camping—camping as we are now in this rest area, without the benefit of the external electricity, piped in water or sewer lines that are available in RV parks. While large fresh and waste water tanks are important, it is the availability of self-generated power that makes dry camping truly possible.

One of the differences between power in our homes and in an RV is that there are several different sources—and kinds—in the RV. Besides propane, (not shown in the above drawing) there's a combination of *AC* (Alternating Current, the kind of electrical current we use at home) and *DC* (Direct Current, the kind a vehicle uses)—and a variety of ways to generate them.

There's the nice big generator Jim liked that provides us with adequate AC power to run our breakfast appliances and our air conditioners. Since it runs on gasoline that is growing more and more expensive, our thrifty souls rejoice that it isn't our only source of power. Rex also has a propane tank and house batteries.

Except for the air conditioners, all of our larger appliances can run on propane. Some, like the fridge, also run on the AC current we get when we plug into power at an RV park. We've added "switch the fridge from electric to propane" to our prepare-for-travel list along with "put up the fridge door bar." Otherwise, our frozen food will thaw.

Rex's two house batteries, not to be confused with the vehicle battery, provide onboard DC power. This type of electricity is not interchangeable with the AC current that we access in RV parks— and use in our homes—although I'm looking forward to when we can use that handy *craigslist* inverter we haven't installed yet to change this DC power to AC.

While the batteries that Rex came with are not the best, they still work and with our other expenses, we hope they will last for a while. We know we are taking a chance. Even when we plug into park electricity, the batteries handle many basic electrical tasks, like the house (interior) lights. More seriously, because our propane appliances use the DC electricity for their cooling fans and circuit boards, they don't run at all without it.

These batteries, like the rechargeable batteries in my camera, must be charged, or filled with power from another source. Our nice big solar panel does this for free—when the sun is shining. However, we've found that whoever installed this after-market addition altered the wiring. Only the solar panel, and thankfully, the engine, now charge the batteries. Not our nice big generator and not the electricity that we pay for when we camp in an RV park. I hope we can change this. It's on my list to talk to my electrician son about when we are in Portland later in the year.

16. The High Life . . . or Not

The next morning we continue west and cross into California. The terrain is still arid, but Joshua trees with their spiny branches dot the high desert now. In Blyth, we pay $4.07 a gallon for gas. Gas is always higher in California than in Arizona, but this is getting ridiculous. It reminds me of my visit to isolated Nome, Alaska, in 2004. Gas sold for $3.49 a gallon; so unbelievably high that I took a photo of the gas station sign for proof. Who knew we'd be buying gas for much more so close to home? Jim happily works the gear shifts as we climb up Cajon Pass. Rex purrs along without a struggle. At the top of the pass, we take Highway 395 toward Mohave.

I'm beginning to feel euphoric. If the RV can climb that steep hill without stalling, surely we've fixed our problem. The road is now fairly level, but the wind is gusting, bending low the grass and brush in our rather arid view. Rex clings to the road without even a minor fishtail. Jim points to a motorhome sitting beside the road. "See, I'll bet that guy had to stop because of the wind. That would be us if we didn't have a tag axle." He grins his big face-filling grin and waves as we sail past the immobile vehicle. Ah, yes! Life is good.

Then it happens. Rex shudders and quits, just like he did south of Tucson. The engine runs, but the wheels don't turn. It's not the hill climbing. We are on flat ground now, not far from Mohave. "Maybe I didn't put in enough oil," Jim says. "I couldn't read the dip stick very well." We both know he's being overly optimistic . . . . he's already added two quarts. I don't argue; I'm still hoping for an easy fix too.

We sit by the side of another two lane road, letting the passing vehicles sway us again, déjà vu. Again we wait. I've become more accustomed to the motion. I don't have to make any quick trips to the bathroom. I've convinced myself that if the cars and trucks zipping by haven't hit us yet, we are probably safe. In fact, we simply sit at the dinette and play cards.

After about twenty minutes, Jim climbs into the driver's seat and turns the key, shifts into drive and steps on the gas. Still back in the dinette, I hold my breath. The engine roars—and then, magically, the wheels begin to roll. Rex moves forward and we are back on the road. I begin breathing again. I can't make up my mind to be thrilled that we are moving again or worried that Rex is still acting up. Maybe it does need more oil.

In Mojave, we stop again for gas. We are getting only seven or eight miles a gallon at best. That's better than the six Jim had warned me it could be. Still, I imagine dimes falling from the exhaust pipe as we drive along; on hills, the dimes turn to quarters or even dollar bills. At this rate, we need to sell lots of programs. So far, we've only been able to sell three. One of those was local and another isn't a sure thing yet.

17. Just a Little Headache

While Jim puts gas in the tank, I get out to use the bathroom. No sense filling up our black water tank when this one's available. The strong wind at my back pushes me along as I walk. On my return, with the wind in my face, every step is a battle. At the door to the motorhome, I struggle to open it against the wind and use both hands to slam it into the latch that holds it open before I climb the two steps to the doorway.

Just as I reach the top step, a gust of wind grabs the door, yanks it out of the latch, and slams it against me. I go flying to the pavement, landing on my rump with the momentum pushing my body backwards. I hear a smushing sound as my head crashes against the pavement. I've just been reading that head injuries are a major cause of dementia. As I lay there afraid to move, I think, "Oh, no, Jim will have to get someone else to do his dementia talks because I'll have dementia myself."

A crowd gathers and someone asks if I'm OK. I move my arms and legs. They feel all right. Nothing's broken. I lift my head. Ow! It hurts. Someone offers to help me up but I decline—it is easier to get myself up old lady style, hands on the ground and my embarrassingly fat bottom rising in the air as I walk my feet close enough so that I can stand.

My fervent prayer is that my contrary bowels won't act up. This time it's flatulence I'm worried about, another not-always-controllable side effect of my abdominal surgery. Please, I pray, not now! For once, my prayers are answered. I don't emit any loud farts or stink up the area. No one even suspects I have such a problem. Thank you, God!

Upright, I decline the offer of an ambulance. "No, I'm fine," I lie. "Just a little headache." All I want is to get back into the motorhome and lie down. I'm not fine, but neither do I want medical treatment. I can think, smile and raise my arms, the required tests in that head injury article. Besides, ambulances and hospitals cost money— money I'd rather spend some other way. I do let someone get ice for my head.

While I lie on our sofa convalescing, with the ice on the bump in my scalp leaking into my pillow, Jim finds an auto parts store and buys more transmission oil. He pours in the whole quart even though from what he can tell, it probably doesn't need it.

As a retired nurse, I know I should have let them take me to the hospital. I've have insisted on it if it had been Jim instead of me! Sometimes, my frugality gets in the way of my good sense.

18. Walmart Wildlife Preserve

We travel along California's more densely populated highways, often separated by red or white flowered oleanders and bordered with the fields of grapevines that climb the low hills. In Fresno, we look forward to our first night in a Walmart parking lot. Alaskans have a saying: "To be a true Alaskan you have to pee in the Yukon, kiss an Alaskan Native and fight a bear." I lived there almost 30 years and never made the grade . . . that bear was just too scary—although on second thought, some of my more disastrous dates might qualify. Alaskan men tend to be awfully hairy.

Anyway, to be a true RVer, you must "drive several miles out of the way to find the cheapest gasoline, own at least two campground memberships and stay overnight in a Walmart parking lot." We have done the first although Jim usually scouts with Froggy first or we check on the internet for the best gas prices. We are halfway to the second with our Happy Camper membership. Now we are going to do the last one. Like good boondockers, we go into the store, buy a few items and check to see if it all right to stay the night.

"Sure," the clerk says. "Park over on the far side of the parking lot. You'll see some other RVs already there."

We take our groceries back to the RV, naturally parked about as far away from the designated parking lot as possible. Jim guides our big awkward motorized box up and down narrow lanes, past cars, trucks, pedestrians and stray shopping carts until he reaches the isolated nether-lands where we set up for the night.

We are pleased to discover that this Walmart offers free entertainment. On the other side of the curb is a field of dirt and weeds, a pile of boards from some long ago project—and a family of prairie dogs. I fix dinner and while we eat, we watch the show. The little rodents dash in and out of their burrows and under the boards. Whenever they hear a foreign sound, they stop in their tracks stand like sentinels, frozen in place. Then at some invisible signal, they all dive into their burrows. After a few minutes of "intermission," they reappear for another "act."

In Stockton, we find huge deciduous trees and small hills. We bite the bullet and park in a regular RV park so that we can go off without worries and leave Rex overnight. My niece Sharon lives about 50 miles away, over tree shaded, two-lane roads that Jim doesn't want to navigate with a cumbersome motorhome. Therefore, we let Rex enjoy the park amenities while we take Froggy, minus the red brake lights that usually decorate its trunk, to Sharon's. We are only staying one night. Jim wants to get to Santa Rosa where we plan to "hospitalize" Rex long enough to have his transmission checked out while we spend several days with his daughter. I'd like to stay longer, but I understand. I, too, want to find out why Rex is balking.

Unlike Jim, who comes from a small family, I have a huge extended family. Although my brother and I are the only ones left in our immediate family, there are cousins, nieces and nephews galore. And then there are my ex-in-laws, my first husband's siblings and families with whom I remain in contact. Wherever I go, I can usually find a relative—or the relative of a relative.

Sharon is my brother George's daughter and only five years my junior. We visit and play "Remember when." Jim sits and listens, entertained by our stories but obviously confused by all the family members we discuss. I have such fun visiting with Sharon that I almost—but never quite—forget my still present headache. I suppose I should have let them take me to the hospital back when it happened. Oh, well. Too late now.

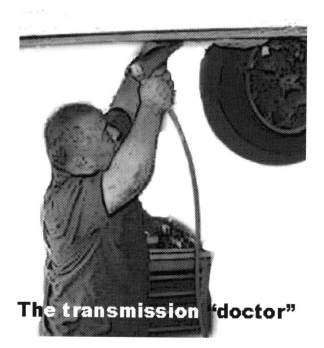

The transmission "doctor"

19. Drive It and See What Happens

Back in Rex with Froggy in tow, brake lights again on his trunk, we continue on towards Santa Rosa and Jim's daughter, Jackie. The scenery gets even greener, but the trees are still mostly deciduous. It's been over two days since Rex has balked. (Of course, one of those days he just sat in Stockton.) Then, only 17 miles from Santa Rosa, it happens again.

It's old hat now. Jim pulls to the side of the road under some welcome shade trees and takes advantage of the wait to take his blood pressure. He tries to do it every morning but this morning he'd forgotten. What with all the excitement and worry, the numbers aren't going down like Dr. Beal wants. However, they're not raising either, so we aren't particularly worried. "The new medication probably needs more time to kick in," Jim says.

As planned, Jim will email his readings to his doctor in a few days. For now, we break out the cards and sit in the shade and play few hands before Jim moves back into the driver's chair. Of course, after its rest Rex moves just fine and soon we arrive at Jackie's.

There's no place to park Rex near Jackie's home, but that's all right. Using the internet, we have found a local transmission shop that works on RVs. We arrange for Rex to be stored there for free during our four days with Jackie and her husband Bill. All we have to pay for this hospitalization is the cost of whatever repairs they do.

We catch up on family news. Jackie, a successful marketing manager who changes jobs like Jim changes socks, excitedly tells us she has applied for a new job. We share what we've been doing on our program. I try to rest when I can so that my headache will go away. Every day it gets a little better, but it's still making itself known—reminding me that just perhaps, my thrifty nature may have backfired and maybe I should have gone to the hospital. Jim keeps track of his blood pressure which continues to plateau.

In the transmission shop, they dump the several quarts of oil Jim has just put into Rex and check for metal particles that would indicate a problem. Two days later, and $175 poorer, we hear the repairman say, "We didn't find anything wrong. I'd suggest you drive it and see what happens."

We leave Jackie's and head north hoping for the best. We travel some 200 miles and congratulate ourselves on how well Rex is behaving. Like the little engine that could, he labors slowly up a hill just outside of Mt. Shasta City. Jim, with his race car driver past, hates climbing hills in a slow moving vehicle. That's why he liked Rex's oversize motor. However with Rex's stopping history in mind, Jim is being patient and not pushing Rex as hard as he might otherwise.

Then it happens. The same thing: the motor is running fine but wheels have stopped turning. Jim manages to get Rex pulled over into a convenient by-pass area for his requisite 20 minute rest.

I take a couple of sodas out of the fridge and Jim breaks out the cards. I'm winning for a change when I see this official looking man walk up to the door and knock. Oh, no. Are we in trouble? Is he going to make us move? If only we could! But the state trooper only wants to know if we need help.

"No," Jim tells him. "The motorhome overheated or something on the hill and we are just letting it cool down." As good an explanation as any—it could even be true. Jim adds, "We'll be moving on very soon." The trouper appears satisfied and leaves. However, the interruption turns my luck. Jim wins the card game.

The scene has changed to mountains now with rocks jutting out in sharp relief and snow covered Mt. Shasta in the distance. Along the road, darker green evergreens are becoming the norm. A far cry from the deserts at home!

We travel now with planned stops every few hours. Jim prefers to choose where we stop instead of letting Rex choose. "We aren't in hurry," we say, as we sit and play our cards, or take a short walk—we need the exercise anyway, we rationalize. Rex behaves and doesn't do any more balking. We seem to have solved the problem.

"I only wish I knew what the problem is that we solved," Jim complains. He's the car guy. He needs to know these things. I'm simply glad we found a solution that appears to be working.

The
Stupid
Button

20. A Proper Shower

We stop in a RV park in northern California. As usual after a day's travel, I look forward to a long hot shower. Rex's stall is a reasonable size but the hot water tank is tiny, thus ablutions must be quick and efficient. When I took my first shower in the RV, I didn't realize that there was a button on the hand-held shower head for turning off the water while soaping down. I'd just lathered up my hair and was about to rinse off when the water quit flowing. I fiddled with the knobs. No water. I was the proverbial "wet hen" and just as mad.

"The dumb shower quit. There's no water coming out." I yell.

Jim comes to my assistance and calmly showed his wet, naked wife that the wand really wasn't broken and that she simply needed to press the stupid button to make the dumb water run again. Even though I can now take a proper shower in the RV, I still prefer to clean up elsewhere.

Of course, using campground facilities can also be challenging. First, most of the shower heads are set so high that a short person can barely reach them to adjust the spray. Of course, that seldom matters, because they are usually not adjustable. What does matter is that by the time the often anemic spray reaches my nether regions, it has weakened even more and cooled down considerably.

I think the campground shower builders take their inspiration from car designers—the ones who make seatbelts to fit tall people. Don't they know that short, chubby women also ride in cars—and take showers? In a car, I've learned to tuck my shoulder strap under my right boob to keep it in place. Left untucked, it crosses over my throat and disappears under my armpit. I live in fear that the belt will strangle me during an accident. As for showers, maybe I should start taking a little stool with me so that I can reach that elusive shower head—but then I'd be afraid I'd stumble and fall off. No, not a good idea.

I gather up my towel and other items and trot over to the clubhouse hopeful that this park provides good showers. They do and I soon get the water adjusted to just the right temperature. I'm standing there blissfully, just soaking up the heat. I pay no attention when someone enters the building. A few minutes later, I also ignore a toilet flushing.

Then "Eeek!" I squeal as I fling myself back out of the way of the now scorching hot deluge. As I stand there, half out of the shower, waiting for it to cool down again, I hardly notice the extra coolness—until I hear a stifled giggle. The flusher has emerged from her stall to face a shower curtain only partially closed on my ample backside. Thank goodness, we both remain anonymous: I didn't see her—nor she, the rest of me.

21. So Sayth the Raven

Marjorie, a big supporter of Jim's charity, the Lewy Body Dementia Association, lives in Bend, Oregon, deep in the mountains of Central Oregon. Therefore we plan to stop a couple of nights so we can meet her. We find a charming RV park, with the camping sites situated in amongst tall pine trees. After a couple days of dry camping, we eagerly anticipate some mindless evenings of cable TV and surfing the internet.

"I'm going to go take a shower," I tell Jim after we set up.

"Didn't your last shower flush you out?" I'd told Jim about inadvertently mooning someone and of course he has to tease me.

"No, not really," I tell him. Park showers are still better than Rex's. I can take as long as I like, use all the water I want, don't have to worry about the hot water running out—and no one is waiting for me to get out so they can use the bathroom. It's worth the challenges.

About half way to the shower building, a raven flies down to greet me. How nice, I think. Even the birds are friendly in this park. And then Raven buzzes me, flying so low I can feel my hair raise in the wind as it passes overhead. I yelp and dodge. This isn't a friendly welcome; this is more like an attack!

As long as I watch, Raven sits on a tree limb and caws. I try to keep watching, but the path is uneven and the minute I move my attention to the ground, Raven buzzes me again. This bird means business! Gratefully, I reach the shower building and escape inside. I take my time and enjoy every moment. No one comes in, so I don't even have to dance out of the way of a toilet-flushing temperature change. My ablutions complete, I exit and find to my dismay Raven is still there, waiting for me.

Raven escorts me back to the RV, playing the same kamikaze game as before. I wave my hands and yelp, but the bird doesn't give up. Is it my imagination, or do the talons get a fraction of an inch closer to my head with each dive? As I duck, flinch and dodge, I am grateful the headaches from my fall over a week ago, always worse when I move my head, are nearly gone. Another less comforting thought follows: What if Raven's talons connect? Will that bring the headaches back? Or even, worse thought, the dementia? Would I even know?

I'm about halfway home when a park employee sees my dilemma and yells at Raven. "That damn bird must have a nest nearby," he grumbles as he walks behind me the rest of the way back to the motorhome.

Raven sits in the tree with an innocent "Who, me?" look. The next day, I forgo a shower.

We enjoy our visit with Marjorie and discuss the idea of presenting programs for nurses in the Bend area. We make some calls and although the nursing school is interested, they tell us their classes are out for the summer. "Can you come back in the fall?" they ask. No, we can't. We have responsibilities in Arizona in the fall.

The next day, our email delivers similar news from the assisted care facility in Spokane, the one where we thought we'd sold a program. "Our staff isn't interested in attending classes in the summer. Can you come in February?" We'd come but we'd have to fly and what they could pay wouldn't even cover our plane fare.

We begin to see that we have two roadblocks: Our subject isn't popular enough to be attractive by itself and the time we want to work isn't when people want to attend trainings. When we presented for free, people weren't so discriminating. Now that we charge, our customers are much more demanding. Looks like we will travel less and park more. Jim, bless his heart, doesn't say a word about how the program isn't paying as well as I'd hoped.

22. Family Confusions

We continue on our way, taking time out for a game of cards every so often and Rex behaves admirably. Our next stop is in Hermiston, Oregon. We are again on flat land. This is a higher, less arid desert than Arizona's. Cottonwood trees, sagebrush and the ubiquitous prickly pear cactus populate the land. We stay at another park in my Happy Camper guide. In most parks, the discount is good for only one night. However, this park allows a hefty four nights at the bargain price. Naturally, we only plan to stay for one. Darn! If our schedule wasn't so tight, I'd be tempted to campaign for another night or two just to take advantage of the bargain.

I went to high school in Hermiston. Shirley, who still lives here, was one of my best friends. I explain to Jim that because my brother George married Shirley's sister, we are both aunts to Sharon, whom we visited in California. Thus, we have always been "shirt-tail" relatives—relatives of relatives. "But Shirley's two daughters are also actual relatives, second cousins, because Shirley married my cousin Cap," I add. By now, Jim is lost. He shakes his head and begs me not to explain anymore.

Cap died well over a decade ago and Shirley soon remarried. We hadn't connected for years. Now, I too have remarried. We enjoy catching up on each other's lives and getting acquainted with our respective "new" spouses.

Cap and Shirley's daughter Vicki also lives in Hermiston. She hadn't been able to meet with us at her mother's, so Jim and I arrange to go to breakfast with her before we leave. The teenaged Vicki I remember is now the mother of two teenagers herself. We discover that we have a special bond. She was very close to her father—and so was I. Although I had a loving father, he was the age of most children's grandfathers. I spent a lot of time at the farm with my aunt and uncle and my cousin, Cap. Twenty-six years my senior, he became my male role model. I even tried to walk like him. Envision an eight-year-old girl in bare feet and a short dress walking behind a man in cowboy hat and boots, stretching to match his long strides. Jim listened entranced while Vicki and I shared "Cap" stories. I am so fortunate that instead of being bored, Jim enjoys our family tales—even if he can't quite figure out who is who.

From Hermiston, we wind up and down over more hills to Spokane, which nestles in a valley that keeps the climate warm. Evergreens of many kinds abound, covering the hills and mountains and filling the valley with greenery. We stop a couple of nights to visit with more shirt-tail relatives. I knew my children's Auntie Jan before I knew Paul—the husband whose hunting plans I spoiled so many years ago. In fact, Janice introduced her brother to me. More explanations about how they all fit into my family from me. More frowns, confused looks and a shrug from Jim, but he enjoys Janice and her husband Bob. We have a good visit.

Bob is retired. Janice, two years my senior, was until she started volunteering in her church office. Before long, they'd hired her to be the church secretary. When we called to say we were coming to visit, and bringing Rex, she said, "The church has a huge lot. If you don't mind dry camping, I'm sure you could stay there."

"Dry camping's easy with Rex," we assure her. And it would save us the cost of city RV parking. We've found that this is usually as high as staying in a motel—and I still have to make the bed! I assured her we'd love to take her up on her offer. Now that we've arrived, we drive into the church lot and look for the office.

"Welcome," Janice says as we come in the door. She's busy, so we don't stay to visit. After she shows us where to put Rex, we make plans to meet later at her home.

We park in the back corner of the church lot—a lone RV in an expanse of concrete. That's our home for the next three days. Because it isn't the weekend, there's no church service, still people come and go. A few teenagers put up a net and play volleyball one afternoon, but no one bothers us.

Except for our overnight in Hermiston, this is the first time we've had with relatives or friends since we left Santa Rosa, where we stayed with Jackie. For the first time we experience staying in Rex while we visit. We love it. We have our own bed. We get up and have breakfast whenever we like. We watch TV—or not. We bask in the joy of being able to visit—and then go home.

This is no small thing. After I sold my condo, we spent a summer visiting friends and relatives. We quickly learned that depending on the hospitality of others, no matter how graciously offered, wasn't for us. It was not the way we want to spend our annual exodus from Arizona's heat. Rex is our answer. Maybe we will eventually tire of this nomadic lifestyle, but for now it is good.

When we leave, Janice is back at work in the church office. We leave a donation with her to thank them for us letting stay in their yard for three days. We may be thrifty, but we know that a donation now will likely pave the way towards another invitation next year—a good investment.

23. Windy Byways

We turn west, headed for Wenatchee where my daughter Leanne lives. The terrain is still hilly, but we are gradually moving lower, into the hot climate of central Washington. We've read about the Petrified Forests in that area and we have the time, so we go the 15 miles out of our way to see them. Our camping book tells us there's a good RV park in the area. We can't find it, but we do see a sign directing us to the Petrified Forest Park.

We drive down a very long winding gravel road and finally come to the entrance to the park. The sign says, "Open 8 AM to 6 PM. It is well after six; we can't even go in and turn around. The road in front of the gate widens enough for a small car like Froggy to turn around, but not Rex. We are stuck unless Jim backs the RV all the way to the main road—and we both know that's not going to happen. Instead, Jim pulls off to the side and we set up camp for the night right behind another sign that says "No Overnight Parking."

No one comes to make us leave, but soon a strong wind starts blowing and we wish we could. Buffeted by the wind, big boxy Rex rocks like a ship on a rough ocean. This is much worse than the swaying caused by large vehicles passing us when Rex balked beside those narrow highways. Jim assures me we are safe. When we go to bed, I try to ignore the wind's wild song as it rocks us into a restless sleep.

We wake to find the rising sun has driven the wind away. A park employee comes and unlocks the gates. We are free to go in, turn around and leave. Of course, we have to tour the visitor's center first. Our guide brings the past to life as she talks about how the forest was petrified. She is another RVer who works for the park and gets to live here for free. Hmm. We could do that! But not now, we have other goals. Jim isn't interested. He comments, "It looks like a lot of work to me."

--Helen's office

Jim's office

Dinette --

24. Offices on the Go

At Wenatchee, we park in front of my daughter's house and go in and greet the family. As usual, Leanne's two teenage boys are busy with their own activities but they do take time to give Grandma a hug. Since Leanne isn't home from work yet, we go back out to Rex. We'll be living in him for the next week, so we have work to do.

First, we must level Rex so we can sleep more comfortably—but more importantly, so that the refrigerator, whose cooling unit requires a level surface, will work properly. When Jim turns on the hydraulic pump to level the RV, the jacks seem stuck. Finally, after a several tries and lots of muscle, they work. I whisper a prayer of thanks—we don't need another crisis.

Our next step is electricity. I bother the boys to ask where we can plug in our long electrical cord. Chris, the oldest, shows me an outlet in the garage. It's Jared's turn on their shared laptop, so he doesn't join us. I plug my end of the cord into the outlet and go see if it works. It does. Better yet, our laptops pick up the wireless connection from the house.

With electricity and access to the internet, we settle in. By the time Leanne arrives home, Jim is sitting at the little table behind the passenger seat, catching up on his hundreds of emails, generated by the online caregiver support groups he monitors. He can turn his easy chair to put his knees under the table or around to face me. I am sitting in my own "office," the dinette, facing Jim, taking advantage of the internet connection to do some research for the book I'm writing on LBD. The dinette seat is firm, a must for my arthritic back, and I have room to spread out my papers.

The printer sits on an ice chest when in use and hides under the sofa the rest of the time. Like our dinner settings, my laptop has its own place mat. This isn't for esthetics, but for efficiency. The mat's slippery surface lets me slide my big 17" laptop over under the window and kazam! The rest of my "desk" is a table for dining or playing cards. I sometimes envy Jim's ability to leave his workspace unbothered but it is very cramped, so the envy doesn't last long.

Wenatchee will soon fill up with family gathering here to celebrate Leanne's 50th birthday. We give Rex a few love pats and tell ourselves how smart we are to come visiting complete with our own living space. We love family, and we look forward to spending time with them. However, we seniors also need "alone time." It is wonderful to have a place where we can entertain, and where we can set our own rhythms—when to get up in the morning, go to bed at night, etc. And we can show off Rex too. He sits in Leanne's yard, behaving well. Of course, we aren't traveling . . .

25. Bargains . . . or Not

Leanne, Jim and I go garage-saleing on the Friday before everyone arrives. Leanne, who learned to like garage sales from me, finds a blouse she can wear to work. I find a long red gel pad, the kind that you use to avoid wrist pain when you type, and it is only a quarter. What a buy!

Then, I spy some glass floats for a dollar each—a great price. These balls, once used on nets by Japanese fishermen, are becoming rare. I stand staring at them, trying to decide if I should add them to the collection I started when I lived in Kodiak, Alaska in the late seventies. The owner sees me debating and makes an offer, "The whole bunch for only $10." There must be more than a dozen in the bucket. It's an unbelievable price. I paid two dollars a ball 30 years ago. I'm on my way to accepting when Jim interrupts.

Early in our marriage Jim assigned himself the job of discouraging me from buying "bargains" that I may later rue. While we are in

Rex, he is especially diligent. I think he has visions of me filling all of Rex's nooks and crannies with my irresistible bargains, weighing him down so that his miles per gallon—and worse yet, his speed on hills will decrease. Now Jim reminds me that I have yet to find a place to display the floats I do own. They are in storage. "You don't need more," he insists.

Sigh. I hate it when he's right. I walk off and leave them. I don't want to weigh Rex down with unneeded purchases either. "But it was such a good bargain," I lament as we climb back into the car. Jim's Cheshire Cat smile about a job well done doesn't make me feel any better.

Back at Leanne's, I take a closer look at my gel pad and find that a small animal has used it for a chew toy. Gel is oozing out of about a dozen tiny holes. Maybe it wasn't such a good bargain after all. Jim shakes his head and suggests I throw it out. Undaunted, I daub the holes with some crazy glue and viola! I have an intact hand rest—a bit rough in spots, but no longer leaking. Triumphantly, it sits like a long red salamander in front of my keyboard and yes, it does keep my wrists from hurting when I type.

Jim's 63 Corvette

26. Flashy Cars

My son Ken and his wife Deb drive up from Portland. My daughter Sue and her husband Randy fly down from Alaska, then drive to Wenatchee in Sue's "new" 1984 tomato-red Corvette.

They recently bought the well-preserved antique and shipped it to Washington so they'd have a vehicle when they are Outside. (To an Alaskan, "Outside," with a capital "O", is anywhere out of the state of Alaska. This refers to a location, not a state of mind—although some Outsiders might disagree.)

Having a husband who loves to drive allowed me to fulfill my dream of traveling in a motorhome. It also means that he loves cars—or for that matter, anything with a motor big enough to drive or fly. I never see him studying literature about them, but he can identify almost any car I point out. It's the same with airplanes or motorcycles.

And so when Sue, with obvious pride, asks Jim if would like to take her 'Vette for a drive, he of course takes her up on her offer. I go along and as we wend through Wenatchee's tree-shaded streets, Jim shares some of his old memories.

He used to own a brand new 1963 Corvette. Red, of course. He wooed his first wife in it. After they married, he drove the sporty little car from Missouri to California, with him and his wife in front and her two school-age daughters crowded into the seat-less back. Jim finishes his story with a laugh, "No way, would I be able, let alone willing, to tolerate two kids for over a thousand miles in such a cramped space now."

I shift around, trying without success to get comfortable in the elderly bucket seat. "I wouldn't want to ride such a long way in this car without kids!"

"Yeah, I don't remember my Corvette being nearly this confining," Jim says as he too, squirms around in a fruitless search for comfort.

"Froggy and even Rex are definitely easier rides," I add.

When we return, Sue generously offers to let Jim have the Corvette all the time she is in Wenatchee. I and my rear are ever so grateful when he politely declines.

Oil under the broken hydraulic jack tubing

27. Playing With Jacks

With the party over, most of the family leaves—jobs beckon. We will leave tomorrow. To facilitate an earlier start, Jim wants to gas up today. However, before Rex can move, Jim must raise the jacks. Remembering the trouble he had lowering them, we hold our breath. When they come up just fine, we both let out sighs of relief.

At Costco, gas now costs $4.17 a gallon. Ulp! But it's the cheapest in town. Higher than it was in Nome, and higher even than the gas was in California. The only bright spot is that when we drive Froggy, which we do except when we are moving from place to place, we get 34 miles to the gallon instead of the eight or less we get with Rex. The little Saturn's tank only holds ten gallons—and we seldom pay more than $20 at a time for gas. In Froggy, we feel like we are traveling almost for free!

We return to Leanne's, and this time, Jim does have trouble with the jacks. In fact, he can't lower them at all. He gets out to look under the RV. "Oh, oh," he says.

Oh, no, this doesn't sound good. It isn't. There's a reddish puddle under a half-lowered jack. "Is Rex bleeding?" I ask, only half in jest.

"Sort of," Jim tells me. He goes on to explain. "It's hydraulic fluid—the oil that makes the jacks work."

Somehow, a hose must have come loose and caught on a jack. That's why Jim had so much trouble lowering them. Raising them was not a problem, but unbeknownst to us, that loose hose dragged the whole five miles to Costco and five miles back. When Jim turned on the hydraulic pump to lower the jacks, all the reddish fluid bled out of the road-worn hose onto the ground. No wonder the jacks don't work!

Our immediate dilemma is how to level Rex. Sleeping on such a slant would not be pleasant with Jim clinging to the edge of the bed to keep from rolling over onto me—and me pushing back to keep from falling out. Even worse, that the coolant in our lovely side by side refrigerator-freezer doesn't work unless the appliance is level. With thoughts of a sleepless night and thawed food, we ask Leanne if she has anything we could put under Rex's back tires.

"No, I don't think so," she says. "But wait! There are some big boards at work. Do you want to go look?"

Of course we do. We three pile into her car—it's bigger than Froggy—and go check out the back yard of the electrical supply store where she is assistant manager. It's after hours, but she has a key. Even so, I look around and hope no one sees us. I feel like a thief, sneaking in where I don't belong. We walk through a yard full of broken equipment over to the side where Leanne points out some heavy timbers. Of varying lengths, each is about a foot wide and almost four inches thick.

Jim nods, grins. "Yes! Those will work."

Yeah, they'll work if we can get them home, I think. I know I can't carry them. But Jim lugs one and Leanne and I together carry another. "Will your boss mind?" I ask Leanne. I'm worried.

"Mom," she says in the same tone I remember using when she was a toddler asking a question for the umpteenth time, "He won't even know, and he wouldn't care if he did. They've been out here for a long time."

Yes, in my concern, I may have asked more than once. I school myself not to ask again. I think she's losing her patience.

The bottom line is that we need those boards and they truly do look like they've been there so long that they've become a part of the environment. Grass was growing over them and other apparently unwanted stuff is beginning to cover them. Even so, I breath a sigh of relief when we get back into the safe territory of her car. At the house, Jim and I get Rex leveled without much trouble and bless those planks.

The next morning, we hook up Froggy and move the boards to the side of the yard where they are out of the way. Although Leanne said that she and the boys can take them back, I don't know if they ever did. Maybe they'll still be there for us to use again next year—if we need them, which I devoutly hope we don't. We add "hydraulic jacks" to our "discuss-with-Bob list" and "emergency blocks" to our list of items to check out at our next Camping World stop.

In our now familiar stop-and-play-a-few-hands-of-cards style, we make it over Snoqualmie Pass without a problem. This is a longer trip than if we'd gone by way of Stevens Pass. However, Snoqualmie's four lane highway cuts through the Cascades in long easy grades. Stevens' two lane highway winds back and forth across the mountains—a fun, exhilarating drive in a car, but not what Jim wants with Rex.

Highway 90 dumps us onto I-405, which takes us north, surrounded by an explosion of greenery clouded by traffic smog. We arrive at BobnIris's in Everett, 30 miles north of Seattle, with nothing new on our fix-it list.

I love Everett's picturesque Victorian homes, many over a hundred years old, that line the streets in the downtown areas. However, BobnIris live in a "newer" part of town, in a duplex with a daylight basement built in 1973. It's a great retirement home for them because the basement rental apartment pays their mortgage. It also has lots of yard space for the multitude of vehicles that Bob, like most mechanics, collects.

28. Good Neighbors

There's plenty of space for Rex, but if we park here, we'll have to move out of the RV. Their yard is far too steep for the leveling jacks. Although BobnIris assure us we are welcome to move into their home for the week we plan to be there, that negates the reason we have Rex in the first place—to be able to live at home wherever we are.

"We could go north to Marysville and stay at the casino," Jim suggests.

"No, that's 20 miles away." I counter. If we were just visiting, that would be bad enough, but "Rex needs to be closer, so Bob can help you with the jobs we've been saving up."

And so, accepting that we must pay the usual motel-high price for urban RV parking, we find a nearby place. When Jim tells me the price will be even higher than we expected, I swallow hard and ask,

"Did you ask if they come in each day to make our bed and leave mints on our pillows?"

Jim shakes his head. I guess that means they don't. He was right. They didn't.

When we return to BobnIris's about noon the next day, Iris has news for us. A neighbor, who is also Iris's hairdresser, has invited us to park in her yard. Julie's place is a short block away. It sounds ideal. Close enough to my family so that we can walk over to visit, and so that Bob and Jim can work on Rex, yet we are on our own.

We go over and check it out. Where my brother's yard slants downward, Julie's large excavated lot is quite flat—perfect for Rex. However, getting long boxy vehicle like Rex in and out of the lot will not be easy. It entails turning down a steep hill and almost immediately turning into the yard. Jim studies it for a moment and nods. He can do it. After all, he only has to do it once—and then of course, in reverse when we leave.

Julie operates her beauty shop out of her home, with customers coming and going continually during work hours. However, there's plenty of room for us and them both. Julie shows us where to park, over to the far side, well out of the way of her customer's cars.

"Do I need to move my car before you drive your motorhome in?" Julie asks. She points with obvious pride to a white sports car.

Jim looks around at the big lot and shakes his head. "No, it's fine where it is. Nevertheless, Julie stands in her doorway and watches nervously while Jim maneuvers Rex into his temporary quarters. I can almost hear her sigh of relief when Jim turns the motor off with her car still untouched by our big monster.

Jim hasn't installed the inverter yet, so we take our laptops to BobnIris's. Even if we can't access the internet, I can work on my book and Jim can review the emails he's already downloaded. My octogenarian brother has a computer but no Wi-Fi. Surprisingly, we find that their renters do—and they are willing to share it with us. Gee! Nice renters!

"What about internet connections?" Jim had asked when we first discussed dry camping. With his load of support group emails, his concern is valid.

"I've researched this," I assured him. After all, I'd miss the internet as much as he would. "The state of Washington has free Wi-Fi in most of their libraries. We just have to find the closest one to wherever we camp." For now we can piggyback on the renter's Wi-Fi. We don't have to go to the library to get our internet fix. We bless the renters.

However, we may not be such good neighbors ourselves. Jim parked Rex close to the fence that separates Julie's yard from a big apartment house. While our generator is very quiet inside, it isn't so quiet outside. We rationalize that because the generator is on the side away from the apartments, Rex and the fence will act as sound barriers when we make coffee and toast at seven in the morning. No one complains, so maybe they really do.

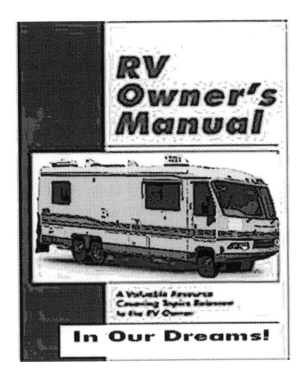

In Our Dreams!

29. Doing Nothing is a Solution

Now that we are in Everett, Jim digs out the list of jobs he's been saving up for Bob's help. the hydraulic leveling jacks take high priority. Although Bob decides that working on them is beyond him, he "knows a guy." When the problem is mechanical, my brother usually does. The men take Rex to see the guy and come back with the problem fixed—for only $30. Would that all our problems could be fixed so cheaply!

We aren't so fortunate with Bob's specialist for the Rex's defunct air conditioner. It takes more equipment to fix than he has available. And he warns us that fixing it will likely be quite expensive. It is raining. Fixing the air conditioner just doesn't seem urgent. We put it on hold.

Next on the list are Rex's house batteries, actually a couple of mismatched car batteries. Bob shakes his head when he sees them. "Using these for your house batteries is like trying to drive a team with a worn out mare and a kid's pony." My brother grew up at a time where driving a team was as common as driving a car—sometimes more so. He goes on to explain, "They are too small and a matched pair is much more efficient." Still, they do the job after a fashion for now. For the time being, we let that purchase wait. Another "do nothing" solution, albeit temporary. We know that unlike the air conditioning which is a comfort issue, new house batteries will eventually become a necessity.

That leaves only the inverter still on the list. Jim hasn't gotten to it yet, although he must before we leave. Neither of us wants to do any prolonged dry camping without the amenities it provides, like powering our laptops and less expensive lighting. The latter is especially important, given the strength of our batteries. Inverter powered AC lights take about half the power of battery powered DC lights.

I help Iris get dinner—pork chops, gravy, potatoes, green beans and bacon with her special, extra rich bread pudding for dessert—heavy food I love but seldom eat anymore—except when Iris cooks it. The men discuss Rex's balky behavior. "Maybe it's vapor lock," Bob suggests.

"No, the motor wouldn't run then and it runs just fine."

"Right. It does sound like an overheating problem though. Hmmm. Perhaps the radiator is too small."

"Yeah, that would do it," Jim agrees.

"Or maybe it's a governor that shuts the transmission off when it gets too hot." Bob looks thoughtful. "No manual, huh?"

Jim shakes his head. When you buy off a sales lot, the previous owner is long gone and you take what you can get; you can't ask them to hunt up the manual. "We've tried to find one," he offers. "Haven't been successful though."

"Probably a good idea to keep trying. The manual might be able to answer your question. My guess is that it isn't anything serious, and that as long as you don't let it overheat, you'll be fine." He holds up his hand in warning, "That's just a guess, though."

"We'll keep looking," I say. I'm usually the one doing Google searches. Then I add with a grin, "In the meantime, we aren't in a hurry to go anywhere and we like to play cards." Hmm, with the air conditioning, that's two problems we've solved by doing nothing!

"Time to eat," Iris announces.

30. Long Distance Doctoring

Jim's blood pressure is climbing. He emails Dr. Beal with his daily readings and, being a methodical person, includes a list of his medications. Turns out, Jim was supposed to continue his old medication AND start the new one as well. The doctor sends a new prescription to the Mesa Costco. Maybe Jim's problem was due to his medication instead of Rex after all!

When Jim picks up his new prescription at the Everett Costco, he looks at it. "Uh, oh," he says, "This is wrong. It should be twice as strong." More phone calls, more emails, and another trip to the pharmacy. Finally, Jim gets the right medication.

While there, Jim asks for the second half of the prescription he could only partly fill in Mesa. "Sure, no problem," the clerk said. But when we go to pick it up, the clerk surprises us with a hefty bill. Turns out the Mesa pharmacist reported the prescription as fully filled. The insurance company won't pay for more until next month. More phone calls, more emails, more trips to the pharmacy. Finally, with only one pill left, Jim gets the rest of his medication. Doing medicine by email is possible, but it sure can be cumbersome!

31. Family Rituals

In Everett, I bask in the feeling of family. With both parents long gone, BobnIris are the closest I have to parents now. Iris serves more of my favorite meals. Bob takes us estate-saleing on Sunday, another ritual, and of course, one that this thrift queen enjoys a lot. Many of the sales are in the older part of town and I get to go inside some of lovely old Victorian homes. I admire beautiful handiwork such as carved door casings and crown moldings—the kind that labor costs make scarce in newer homes. Jim goes along, mainly, I suspect, to govern my purchases. I find a few things for Rex's kitchen and better sheets for the bed.

Jim is excited to find some boards that will work as levelers if we ever need them again. "They are almost free—a much better buy than those plastic things at Camping World."

"And way heavier too," I point out. Jim grins, shrugs and buys them anyway. Apparently weight matters less when it is something "important." It takes both men to tote the planks to Bob's car and later, store them in one of Rex's basement compartments.

"Look here," Bob says as he shows me an old set of dominos. "These are only a dollar." I'd mentioned earlier that I was looking for some.

"The dots are all one color," Jim observes, doing his usual "curbing-her-buying" act. "They'll be hard to read." True, but they are the thick-edged, hard-to-find kind and, besides I have a plan.

When we return, Iris and I get out her fabric paints and we spend the afternoon painting. When we finish, I have a set of dominos with the spots of each denomination painted a different color. The best part: they only cost me a dollar—and a fun afternoon's work.

In the evening, my nephew and his family from down the road come over and we play Mexican Train with my "new" dominos. On other nights we play a variety of card games, all pastimes I learned from BobnIris and now share with Jim.

Let there be light

32. Bargains Revisited

Up to now our dry camping has been for only one or two days at a time. Five days into our stay in Everett, we add another fact to our growing store of knowledge about dry camping: the length of one's stay depends on the size of one's holding tanks and Rex's limit is less than a week. Jim calls me from the bathroom, where he is taking his morning shower, "My shower water isn't draining."

Oh, no, I think. "Is the pipe plugged?"

"No, the gray tank is full." He's out of the bathroom now, modestly covered by his towel, checking the array of monitors above the microwave that tell us how full our holding tanks are. I'm tempted to tease him by yanking the towel. I resist. I don't think he is in a playful mood.

"The black tank is nearly full and our fresh water tank is almost empty," he says as he pushes buttons and reads the gauges. The towel is slipping—maybe if I give it just a little help? He returns to the bedroom before I get up the nerve. It's just as well. Jim doesn't tease well when he's busy.

Like a five-year-old hopping on one leg, Rex needs to "go." *Now.* If we were in an RV park, our present crisis would be no big deal. Jim would simply go out and open the proper valve to drain the tank. Of course, he'd dress first.

Here it isn't quite that easy; Rex has to travel to a dump station. There's a rest area only a few miles away with one. Sure, it takes more effort but I don't see a real problem. We just pull out of Julie's lot and drive to the rest area. We don't even have to hook up Froggy. However, Jim is frowning—he must see something I don't.

At least, I don't until I look out the window. Several cars whose owners are here for their usual Saturday hairdo block our way out of Julie's yard. Now I'm frowning too.

While Jim dresses, I go over to Julie's busy shop. There appears to be a party going on, complete with snacks and soda. Women sit with their hair in various stages of dress, others are waiting their turn and I recognize Julie's sister who is simply visiting. A fluffy white, beribboned dog stretched out on the floor wags her tail and a big gray cat winds around my legs.

Interrupting the party, I apologize and explain that we need some cars moved. I assured Julie that Jim doesn't need her to move her sports car but she moves it anyway. "Just in case," she explains with a nervous smile. I don't think she trusts my husband to see her precious little car when he is driving monster Rex.

There's also the problem of that zigzag hill climb we'll have to do to get out and the other equally difficult maneuver to get back in. At the start of our week, the effort was worth having such a good place to stay. Now Jim is seriously considering other options.

We could just leave, but we plan to spend time boondocking in casino parking lots and Jim has yet to install the inverter. Even he doesn't want to leave without it. Moving back into that high priced RV park where we stayed the first night in Everett isn't an option that our frugal souls can abide. Jim voices a third option, "We could move up to the casino in Marysville. It will only be a couple of days."

I shake my head. I really want to be where Bob can help with the inverter if necessary. Jim sighs and agrees to stay. I think he likes the idea of backup support too.

We make it out of Julie's lot without hitting anything and drive to the rest stop, where we go through the dump and fill process. Julie only works until noon on Saturdays, so if we wait until after that to return, it will be much easier to get back into our corner. A few hands of cards while we sit in the rest area get us past the witching hour. Back at Julie's, Jim manages to guide Rex through the downhill zigzag back into the lot. It doesn't take us long to get resituated. As we had hoped, all the cars are gone, even, I notice with a smile, Julie's.

The next day, Jim finally tackles the inverter. It doesn't work. Bob checks the wiring and says it's the inverter, not Jim. Sigh. No wonder I got it at such a good price on *craigslist* back in Mesa. Too late, I remember an important rule for secondhand buying: "Always check out your merchandise while you can still return it." We go to a local hardware store and find a similar inverter on sale. However, the salesman encourages us to buy a smaller one. "Overkill," he says about the one we planned to buy. Where was this wonderful guy when we were buying our last car? We ended up with a bunch of stuff we didn't need because, the salesman insisted, "It's always easier to buy it now than add it later."

We thank the nice man and take the smaller inverter home. Jim installs it beside the still mismatched batteries and rigs up an inside switch. He's so proud of his job that he walks the half-block over to BobnIris's where I'm visiting with Iris, "Come see," he insists. Back in the RV, he shows me the switch, hiding behind the sofa. "Flip it," he says.

I do, and Voila! A little nightlight plugged into an outlet beside the switch comes on. "Wow!" I say as I flip the switch a few more times and watch the light flash off and on. Such a handy husband I have!

For the next few weeks, we plan to dry camp at several Indian owned casinos in northwestern Washington that encourage free parking in hopes that the campers will spend the money—and more—gambling instead. With gas so high and our program on hold, we need to save money where we can.

With most of our list of questions for Bob at least addressed if not solved, our week in Everett is over. I hug my family one more time and tell them goodbye. We give Julie a thank you note and some money—and ask if, next year, we can arrange to plug into her electricity. That will eliminate some of our power problems—and some of the noise as well. No one at the apartment house has complained, but I'm sure they'll be glad to know she is willing to supply us with the small amount of power we need.

33. Casino Capers

Our destination this first day is a casino in the far northern part of the state. We arrive late in the afternoon and find the designated RV area.

"It looks full," Jim says. It sure does.

"We just got our first lesson about casino parking," I comment as we drive around futilely looking for an empty space.

"Huh?" Jim doesn't understand.

"I mean that we need to arrive early, before the evening rush."

We take one last hopeful pass through of the area. Then Jim shrugs, "Oh, well, there's always Walmart." We'd passed one only a mile or so back.

"If we'd wanted to park in there, we didn't have to drive a thousand miles. We could have stayed in Mesa." I grumble.

"Yeah, well, at least it's free."

And noisy too. Their RV area is as usual at the far edge of the lot—right next to a busy road. With all the trees around one would think Walmart might plant some as a sound barrier between the lot and the highway. But then, I doubt that they want to do anything that would make our stay pleasant enough to entice us to stay longer than a night or so. There aren't any cute rodents to entertain us either.

We breakfast early and arrive back at the casino before ten the next morning. It pays off. We find a spot.

"I'm sure glad we don't have to stay at Walmart another night," Jim says. "It was almost as noisy as that truck stop south of Tucson."

"Yes, it was sort of like trying to sleep inside the casino," I agree. I'm not a fan of casinos. Too much noise and hype. A half hour, and I'm ready to leave. Besides, our frugal nature makes it difficult to enjoy feeding all that money to machines with so little return. I don't think we are the kind of folks they are trying to attract with their free camping spaces.

Setting up for dry camping is usually quite simple, unlike preparing to leave which isn't much different no matter where we are. We park so there is space for both Rex and Froggy. Then we get Rex as level as we can—an easy job now that the jacks work. That's it! We don't even have to unhook if we aren't planning to take the Saturn anywhere. I'm ready to sit back and enjoy our home on wheels, but Jim is eager to be out and about. His father was born near here and he wants to see if he can find any family information in the local museum.

We have Froggy unhooked and are almost ready to leave when a shiny diesel pusher towing a late model Lincoln SUV pulls in next to us. A "pusher" is a diesel-powered motorhome—more expensive but more power-efficient than a gas-powered unit like Rex. This one is big, and new. It probably cost more than a nice suburban house and the SUV alone probably cost as much or more than our manufactured home back in Mesa. A couple about our age climbs out of the pusher at the same time we exit Rex. We wave and stop to talk for a moment.

"Going to go try your luck in the casino?" I ask.

"Aw, we may go in and walk around some," the man answers. He's dressed casually, but the fit of his clothes say they came from a high-end store.

His wife, in comfortable but equally expensive-looking clothes adds, "We really aren't fans of casinos. They are much too loud. We just stay here because it's free."

Hmm, where have I heard that before? It makes sense for us, with our second hand motorhome and limited budget. But these apparently wealthy folks? Well, maybe that's why they're wealthy.

"Yeah, we almost never stay anywhere that we have to pay. There's usually some place where we can stay for free or for very little," her husband says with a proud grin.

I'm amazed. We've been talking about buying a RV park membership so we can have nicer places to stay and they, with their apparent affluence, want to boondock all they can.

We say goodbye and they head towards the casino for their obligatory "walk around." We drive away in our little old Saturn.

"Maybe," Jim suggests as we head out on our search for evidence of his family, "They are spending their money on RV and car payments instead of nice places to park." Yes, buying second hand has advantages. As long as Rex behaves, we do have funds left for other things.

Bald or shaved,
Norwegian or Finnish,
About the same to me

34. Digging for Roots

On the way to the picturesque village of La Conner, we admire the flower fields. Splashes of color as far as the eye can see: red and gold tulips, purple uh, some kind of flower, and some white daisies. In town, we wander through shops with beautiful glassware and pottery. I admire but I don't buy. The prices are higher than this second-hand Nora can consider. And besides, like the glass balls at the garage sale in Wenatchee, I really have nowhere to put them. Certainly not in Rex, and not in Mesa either. I'm glad I down-sized when I moved to Arizona, but there's a price.

In the museum, a friendly docent helps Jim look for family history. I see a bald man in a diorama about early Finnish settlers that looks promising. "Look here," I tell Jim. "Doesn't that man look like you?

Jim looks closely at the picture. "No, I don't think so. He's bald. I'm not bald; I just keep my hair cut short."

I grin. "Not short—shaved." He cuts his own hair and keeps it short enough you can see his scalp. "I still think he looks like you. Maybe he's a relative."

Jim is affronted. "I'm Norwegian, not Finnish."

I shrug. Finnish, Norwegian, whatever. All of those pale people look the same to me, against my darker French-Indian heritage. I still think that bald head really does look like Jim's shaved one.

The day ends on a sad note for Jim because that is as close to finding any of his relatives as we came. At the least, he'd hoped to find something about his grandfather. It isn't an unrealistic expectation. The man helped to start more than one college in Washington. We look. The docent looks. There is no mention of Whitworths in their records.

Bingo and his generous owner

35. Inflation

The next day we return home from an internet fix at the local library to find one of Rex's back tires is low. No problem—our motoring plan covers RVs too. After a couple of calls back and forth, they say they can find no one in our area who is willing to come fix a motorhome tire. However, they'll refund up to $260 if we find someone to do it and submit the bill. "$260 to inflate a flat tire?" I ask, my voice rising in disbelief. What have I gotten us into?

Jim decides to try fixing it himself with the tiny compressor he keeps in Froggy, the one he uses to inflate my bicycle tires. It will be a long process: ten minutes pumping and ten minutes to rest the compressor, per instructions, but he says, "I've got more time than money."

A man in baggy overalls and a scraggly beard ambles over with his slow, fat dog. "You're welcome to use my big compressor," he says.

"That's kind of you," Jim says. But, like most men, he hates asking for help, or apparently, even taking it when offered. He indicates the little compressor that's on break while they talk, "This is working. It's slow, but I'm not going anywhere."

"Well, if you need it, feel free to come ask. I'm right over there." He points to an aged maroon and once-white Fleetwood motorhome in the next row. The man stays to talk. "About a year ago I lost a tire on the freeway," he volunteers. "It got so low that it wore out before I could make it somewhere to get it inflated. I went right down to Sears and got me a compressor so's I wouldn't get caught that way again." He grins. "I wasn't going to buy such a big one, but this one was on sale, so I got it." The dog starts straining on his leash. "All right, Bingo. I know. It's feeding time, isn't it?" The man follows Bingo who is waddling off towards home, and his food dish.

Jim starts up his little compressor for another ten-minute cycle. After several more of these, he succeeds in getting the tire pumped up. "And it didn't cost any $260 either," he brags.

The next morning, Jim gives me the bad news. The tire is even lower than it was before.

"And the air bags are low too," he adds. "So low that the chassis is brushing the tires."

"Air bags?" I ask. Aren't air bags in steering wheels and dashboards? Why would they be causing the chassis to brush the tires?

Jim explains, "All large motorhomes have air bags over the rear axles to assist the shock absorbers and springs. They make Rex ride easier."

"Oh," I say. This is beginning to sound serious. We certainly can't move Rex until we get the chassis off the tires. I'm wondering how long it will take to blow up giant air bags with that dinky bicycle pump from Froggy. A week? A month?

"Blowing up the bags is supposed to be automatic," Jim anticipates my question about the little compressor.

Uh, supposed to be? This still isn't sounding good.

He points to a knob on the dash, "This button is connected to a compressor under the hood that pumps air into the bags. "But, see . . ." He pushes the button. "Nothing happens."

I sigh. I was right. Not good. This is beginning to sound expensive. A lot more than $260.

"However, there is an emergency system for manually inflating the air bags," Jim tells me.

Ahh! That's better. Of course, now we are back to trying to inflate giant airbags with a bicycle pump.

It's Jim's turn to sigh. "I guess I'll go see if Bingo's owner will loan me his compressor after all."

Our neighbor is outside on his cell phone, so Jim sits playing with the air bag button while he waits. I go do dishes. With a motorhome, you have to do housework even on vacation. Pretty soon, I hear, "Hey!" I run up front to see what's happened.

Jim is beaming. "I got the air bags to work. See this button?" He points to a button above the one he had been pushing earlier.

"Uh-huh," I say. There are several buttons on the dash. The whole array looks like Greek, Russian, Yupik, anything but English to me. How does he know what any of them do?

Jim explains. "When I push this one, the compressor works." He points to the button he'd been pushing earlier, "This one is to let air *out* of the bags." No wonder the air bags were sagging onto the chassis!

Whew! Again I wish for an instruction manual. It would have made things so much simpler. Nevertheless, we are relieved that Jim has figured it out.

Our neighbor finishes his call and soon he and Jim and Bingo are standing in male camaraderie beside Rex silently watching the big compressor put air in our tire. Finished, the man takes his compressor home with our profuse thanks and some table scraps for Bingo. Jim comes inside and shows me a damaged tire valve cap. "I think this was causing the leak," he says. The next morning he checks the tire. It's still up. We contemplate buying a larger compressor. We certainly can't count on the kindness of other campers all the time.

36. No Rest for the Deserving

A few days and another casino parking lot later, it begins to rain. It pours down like it often does in the Northwest where rain, heavy rain, is a fact of life year round. No matter. We are ensconced in our respective work stations, listening to the cozy patter of raindrops on our roof while we enjoy our laptops. My cold feet remind me that it's getting chilly, so I get up to turn on our gas furnace. First, I check the needle on the battery gauge. As I feared, it is too low to start the furnace, or run the fan once it starts. Our lovely solar panel isn't providing enough power to charge them. However, all is not lost. We can still use Rex's engine to give them a boost. Thus, I will have to start the motor to charge the batteries to run the furnace to warm my feet. I get up from my "office" at the dinette and squeeze past Jim in his work station just behind the passenger seat.

As I bend over the driver's seat and reach out to turn the key, I exclaim, "I felt a drop of water on the back of my neck!"

"You better be imagining it." Jim doesn't even look up. He is enjoying our rare respite, where everything seems to be working.

I feel another drop. "Sorry, dear. I'm not imagining it." I point to a dark spot on the carpet right under where I felt the drip.

This time Jim looks. Then he groans. I find a bowl and he puts it under the drip. An additional "plop" makes a tympanic counterpoint to the now less cozy sound of the rain on our roof.

We go through the process of starting the furnace without further problems and settle back into our respective spaces. But the mood is spoiled.

I break the uneasy silence to say what we are both thinking—and dreading, "We should see about fixing the roof."

Jim looks at the water washing down Rex's windows and groans again. He hates getting wet. He even uses an umbrella with a soft warm sprinkle—the kind that's fun to walk in. I'm not sure why . . . he doesn't have hair to get wet. "But you like to shower," I argued once. "That's different," he told me flatly. End of discussion. He hates being out in the rain. Nevertheless, he will be the one getting up on the roof—in the rain, if necessary—and fixing the leak. My balance is not nearly good enough. Besides, he's the man. (Yes, I'm a modern woman, except for sometimes . . . .)

We brave the rain and drive to a nearby town to get supplies. It turns out that what we need depends on the kind of roof we have. If we use the wrong kind of sealant, it will eat into the roof. "What kind of roof do you have?" the salesman asks.

Jim and I look at each other. "A rounded one," I volunteer. Versus the kind with square edges, I mean.

The man's eyes all but roll. I don't think that was the right answer. "Is it rubber?" He asks the stupid lady. Jim and I both look blank.

"How old is it? When was it made?" The questions come quickly one after the other. I think the salesman is getting impatient with these motorhome newbies.

"It's a 1994," Jim answers, obviously glad to finally have an answer for the man.

"Well, that's right in the middle of the time when most roofs were made of rubber."

OK. Then we just buy the stuff for fixing rubber roofs. Of course that kind is twice as expensive as the others.

"But," he continues, "Maybe they used something else on yours. You really need to know." He looks at Jim. "Have you been up on the roof?"

"Yeah, well, I climbed up this morning, and looked at it."

"Did you touch it?"

"Uh, no, I was hanging on to the ladder." Jim holds up two tightly clasped hands as though hanging on to a ladder for dear life. No, he wasn't frightened, but remember everything was WET. Jim was probably trying not to touch anything he didn't have to.

However, our salesman doesn't know about Jim's aversion to water. The man gives him an evaluating look and says, "You do know you'll have to get up there and walk on the roof to fix the leak, don't you?"

Jim nods. "I can do that," he says. He could have added, "when the sun is shining," but he didn't.

I'm glad he isn't afraid to go up on the roof, because I doubt that I could. Not only is my balance uncertain, unlike Jim, I AM afraid of heights. My daredevil kids used to accuse me of being irrationally afraid for them to stand near cliff edges or climb high ladders—like the woman who puts a sweater on her kid when SHE is cold.

The salesman gives Jim one more look. I perceive an invisible not-my-problem shrug as he moves on and reaches for a tube of caulking, "Here. You can use this on any surface. The old seams often become cracked and that's probably where your problem is. If you spread this over the area, it should seal any leaks."

We buy the caulking he recommends. Back at the RV, the rain has stopped so Jim goes out. I hear him walking the length of the roof. I don't watch, but I have my cell phone handy to call 911 if he falls. A few minutes later, I hear steps going the other way. Soon he is back inside—without falling. "There were cracks, just like he said there would be." Jim holds up the half used tube like a trophy. "And I fixed them."

"Did you check any other seams? Like the vents?" I'm hoping he doesn't have to do this more than once.

"Yeah, I checked. The only place that might need it is near the bathroom vent." Jim looks out at the cloudy sky. "But I didn't do it now. I wanted to get down before it began to rain again." I don't especially want him up there at all (my mother-with-the-sweater-complex) and certainly not in the rain, so I don't argue.

We had picked up some VCR tapes at a thrift shop when we were in town so after supper, we plug one in and enjoy watching Babe win prizes and solve mysteries. We weren't sure the inverter would power the VCR and the TV together but it does—and without the expense of running the generator. Wow! I think. All the luxuries of home!

The next day the sun is shining. Jim climbs up on the roof again. In less than fifteen minutes, he climbs back down with a satisfied grin and a nearly empty tube of calking. Mission accomplished.

After an enjoyable Sunday spent doing more exploring, we dig out another thrift store video and pop it in the VCR. We sit comfortably ensconced on chair and sofa, eating popcorn, drinking soda and watching *Notting Hill*. Just as Hugh Grant is discovering the downside of loving Julia Roberts, the screen goes blank and our lights die. Rudely thrown back into reality, I reach behind me and flip the inverter switch. Nothing happens except that my popcorn spills all over the floor. I clean up the popcorn—and grumble about Rex and his contrary ways.

Jim gets up and fishes a flashlight out from the cupboard over the driver's seat. He's grumbling too, "I'll have to go outside and try to reset it there." It's after 10 and Jim hates working without good illumination almost as much as he does getting wet. This is more understandable however. He doesn't see well in dim light. Unlike Jim, I can see fairly well in the shadows. I'd go but I wouldn't know what I was supposed to do. And besides, he's the man . . . .

Ouch!" I hear him say once. There's a bit of a scuffle, an unrepeatable word or two and then, nothing. But he is back before I start to worry.

"What happened," I ask. "Did you fall?"

"No, I just stumbled on a rock." He slumps down on the sofa. "And then, when I sat the flashlight down so I could unlock the compartment, I could barely see what I was doing. It was like trying to give a horse an enema in the dark. I thought I'd never get it open." I think my urban husband has been around my farm-raised brother too long. I'm beginning to feel guilty about not volunteering to go. "But," he continues, "I finally got it unlocked. Not that it helped. I pushed the restart button and nothing happened." He sighs. "Looks like the inverter overloaded and shorted out." Head held up by his hands, he sits under a black cloud of depression. He'd be crying but of course, men don't cry . . . .

I plop down beside him and join the pity party. I'm not thinking such nice thoughts now about that salesman who talked us into buying smaller. In fact, I'm wishing he'd kept his big fat mouth shut.

In the morning we go buy a third, and this time, larger inverter.

On the way home, Jim glances at me and comments, "Have you noticed that what we've saved by not staying in RV parks with all the amenities, we're spending on equipment so we can camp in gravel parking lots?"

"Oh, well, it's an adventure," I say with a false smile.

"Yeah," Jim says with no smile at all. I suspect that right now he'd prefer some of those RV park amenities to a new inverter—especially one he'll have to install.

Back at the motorhome, Jim soon has inverter number three wired in and working. That evening, we finish the movie and watch Hugh Grant and Julia Roberts make a go of it after all.

"Not Happening"

37. Going South

Gas is getting cheaper—Froggy's last fill-up was under four bucks a gallon. "I never thought I'd consider $3.97 a gallon cheap!" I comment.

A few days after the roof episode, I say to Jim, "Have you noticed we haven't had a crisis lately?" "Shhh," Jim says as he pulls into yet another casino parking space.

Life is good. Rex is every bit as comfortable as we'd hoped. The new inverter is working well. I'm on one of the final chapters of the book I'm writing about Lewy body dementia.

"Shh," Jim says again. "Don't tempt the devil, uh Rex."

I grin. Yes, Rex does seem to be devilish . . . especially when he quits running at inopportune times. He is also home to the nomads we've become. With gas so high, we probably couldn't give him away, let alone sell him. We might as well learn to love him, devil or not.

We are as far north as we plan to take Rex and now it is time to backtrack. It will take us over a week to wend our way south to Portland. We plan to spend another week there touching bases with my son and some friends before we fly to Alaska to visit Sue and Randy.

We stop at the casino in Marysville for a night—the same one we rejected on our way north. This time, we aren't planning to do any visiting. We'll do that tomorrow when we get to Everett. But Marysville has some good outlet stores—and the required Walmart, of course.

Outlet stores serve a double purpose. We enjoy looking for bargains on new items, of course but we also like to walk around. In Alaska, the big malls open their doors at 6 am in the winter for "mall walkers," seniors who needed a safe, warm place for their morning constitutionals. Our walks at outlet malls serve a similar purpose. Because of our sedentary ways, we've found that exercise is a major issue for us. In Mesa, I ride my three-wheeled cycle and swim. Jim plays golf. I left my cycle in Mesa and casino parking lots seldom have swimming pools or golf courses. Well, I do get a little exercise every morning when I make up that walk-around bed, but that's not enough.

In the evening, after we've worn ourselves out walking around the outlet stores, we check to see if anything is on our inverter-powered TV. Like our power and water, Rex has two sources for TV reception: the cable we find at most RV parks and an antenna that stores flat on top of the roof. Cable TV is another amenity that casino parking lots don't provide but there's' still Rex's antenna. Sometimes, a scan will find one or more broadcast channels. If it doesn't, that's when we watch one of our movies. Jim flips a switch from "cable" to "antenna" and, using the handle in the ceiling over his work station, he cranks up the antenna so that it is standing straight and tall. This evening, we are in luck—the scan shows a couple of stations. The two of us kick back, chow down on popcorn and watch Jeopardy. Then one of our favorite reality shows entertains us until bedtime.

The next morning, we eat breakfast and are ready to leave by 9 am. As Jim drives Rex out of the casino parking lot, I notice several people waving at us. I smile and wave back. "The folks around here sure are friendly," I remark.

We pull out on the highway and almost immediately, have to stop for a red light. A car pulls up next to us. The passenger has her window down and is pointing and yelling. Jim rolls his window down and she yells again, "Your antenna! It's up."

The light changes and we have to go. But Jim waves his thanks and pulls over as soon as he can. Sure enough, the antenna is still up—and it's in tatters. Jim goes back into the RV and cranks it down—too late to do much good, but at least the damage is out of sight now.

I suggest we use a pink twister, a patio ornament I picked up in a dollar store, to remind us the antenna is up.

Jim watches me hang the plastic spinner from the antenna crank to show what I mean, and shakes his head. "It's right over my desk," he complains.

"But we'd only hang it there when we are using the antenna."

He eyes the offending spiral warily, as though it were a deadly icicle about to fall and skewer him, and shudders. I take pity on my paranoid husband and let the idea, good as it is, go. We add "check antenna" to the prepare-to-leave-list.

We plan to stop in Everett for a couple more nights. We are staying at a Walmart this time; it's much easier to access than Julie's place. Besides, we need to buy a new antenna.

The finale of our favorite reality show is tonight and Jim is sure we should be able to access it via our TV—if we can replace the antenna. In the RV section of the store, we rejoice to find one that should work just fine.

Jim takes another walk on Rex's roof while I hide inside, silently urging him to quickly finish his job and climb down to safety. About 15 minutes into the ordeal, I hear something come crashing down. I dash outside, fearing I'm going to find my husband crumpled on the pavement. Instead, I see the old antenna where Jim had tossed it down. When I can breathe again, I laugh. I should have known Jim would have made a bigger thud than it did, but who was thinking?

Back in Rex, Jim runs the scanner and the right station shows up. We have TV! We take a salad over to BobnIris's and have dinner with them but don't stay to visit afterwards. They have a meeting they must attend this evening, so we are on our own. That's fine— we have that reality show to watch.

The next night, Friday, my nephew Roy and his family show up at BobnIris's after supper. We end up playing Mexican Train well past my bedtime of 10 pm. Back home, Jim, who seldom goes to bed until after midnight, turns on the TV. I tell him good night—I'd fall asleep on the sofa if I tried to watch. I'm much more comfortable in my bed.

I've just dozed off when I hear him yell, "Helen! Wake up. We have to leave."

"Huh?" I'm not really coherent yet. Nor do I want to be.

"We have to leave," he repeats. "The news guy on TV is saying that the road between here and Renton is going to be blocked all weekend, starting at 5 a.m. tomorrow morning."

"So?" I know there's more than one way south. I pull the covers over my head.

Jim won't leave me alone. "The detour will take us right through Seattle."

I sigh. Driving through Seattle during rush hour isn't fun for anyone and especially not for someone driving a big RV. "OK," I moan as I throw the covers back and get dressed.

Preparation to leave can take up to an hour, depending on how rushed we feel. It is quite involved, after all. We've learned by experience that when we move Rex, anything loose takes on a life of its own. Unsecured sliding closet doors slam back and forth, drawers not firmly pushed in and unlatched cupboard doors fly open and disgorge their innards, the unlatched bathroom door flaps open and slams shut—but never latches. If we forget to move the dish drainer from the counter to its berth in the kitchen sink, the first sharp turn will send it flying onto the floor with a crash. And the antenna, of course. The *new* antenna. I double check to see that it is down.

Outside, Froggy waits for hookup. I do the inside stuff and am out the door, ready to help Jim by the time he gets the Saturn jockeyed around behind Rex. Tonight, impelled by the promise of bed as soon as we find a place to park in Renton, we pull out of the parking lot in a record twenty minutes from when I got up. Around midnight, we pass the to-be-blocked-off area and soon after that, enter the city limits.

We check our off-the-internet list of Walmarts. There's one here and we soon find it. We see other RVs already parked in the lot and so we gratefully "drop anchor" and go to bed. In the morning, we take our time getting breakfast and eating. There's no rush now that we are past the road work. Dressed and full of a good breakfast, we exit the motorhome to go visit the store and buy a few things as a way of thanking Walmart for their hospitality. And there, on the pole right in back of Rex is a sign. "No Overnight Parking."

We didn't see it when we parked. Really, we didn't.

38. Power Struggles

We stop in Auburn, at another casino. We plan to be here for several days. It's a fairly central place and we don't plan to be in the Portland area until late next week.

Once we get Rex leveled, I start dinner. I switch on the generator so I can use the microwave to cook my casserole. Even though we don't use it for much more than breakfast coffee and toast, the big generator was one of Rex's selling points. It has the kind of power Jim revels in. I like it because it runs so quietly we can hardly hear it.

"Do you want more casserole?" I ask Jim. We are sitting at the table, replete with food. He shakes his head. It would have been his third helping, so I'm not surprised. I don't want any more either. It was good, but I made too much. Oh, well, it will work for one more meal. I'd get up and start doing dishes, but I'm too relaxed.

Suddenly the sound of a motor that seems to be shuddering as it grows louder blasts away the quiet. Then abruptly, the noise ends. The whole sequence takes maybe thirty seconds. By the time we realize that the racket comes from Rex, there is only silence. Startled, we look at each other.

"The generator!" Jim's shouts. With no sound to remind me, I'd forgotten to turn it off before we sat down to eat. He jumps up, goes over and pushes the generator's start button on the dash. Nothing. He pushes again with the same result, then heads for the door. I follow, not that I really think that I can help.

It is still light, so he doesn't have to fumble around getting to the restart button on the generator itself. I thank God for small favors; but those favors are limited. Again, nothing happens. We both stand there staring at one more offending piece of equipment.

In the next space over, a man with dark curly hair that's about three haircuts too long exits from a small well-worn travel trailer parked behind an equally old and battered pickup. He's wearing a tee shirt that emphasizes his bulging muscles while advertising Budweiser, sharply creased jeans tight enough to advertise his manhood and fancy scroll-worked two-tone cowboy boots. "Generator trouble?" he asks?

Jim nods. "Yeah.

"I heard the noise."

Yeah, him and everyone else in the parking lot! It was so loud that before I realized it was Rex, I'd had visions of a plane crashing on us.

The guy puts on the western hat he's been carrying and manages to squat down without bursting his jeans. He looks closely at the generator for a moment before getting back up. Then he and Jim stand together quietly, as men often do, just looking. Eventually, our neighbor offers, "I'm a mechanic. You want help? I've worked on this same brand.

"Yeah, looks like I need it," Jim nods but he is not smiling. I can see the dollar signs adding up behind his eyes.

Another minute of silence ticks by and then the man responds. "Well, the wife and I are going to the casino this evening and we have to do errands in the morning, but how about tomorrow afternoon?"

The wife is standing in the doorway of their trailer. She's a tiny bird-like woman with too many face wrinkles for her jet black hair to be real. Dripping in gold-colored jewelry and dressed in spandex jeans, psychedelic tie-dyed blouse and sandals with three-inch heels, she is ready to go try the slots. So some people who park in casino parking lots actually do spend time and money in the casino! She negotiates the two steps to the ground without tripping, and minces over to join us.

We all introduced ourselves—the man's name is Hank and hers is Alice. After a few moments of chit-chat, we set up an appointment with Hank for sometime after three tomorrow.

Hank shows up on time, and quickly gets to work. Today he is in a chambray work shirt and comfortable blue jeans. An oily baseball cap attempts unsuccessfully to tame his longish hair. He squats down and looks at the generator again, pushing this and nudging that. After only a few minutes, he points to a piece of equipment behind the generator, "That's the fuel pump, and I'll bet it's your problem."

Jim nods as though he knows what the man is talking about. Maybe he does.

Hank pulls a pair of pliers out of his pocket and gives the pump casing a couple of hard taps. "OK," he says, "Start it up."

Jim pushes the start button on the generator—and it runs!

With a satisfied grin, Hank stands up and points his pliers towards the pump. "If it chokes again," he says, "just give a few good taps before you do anything else." Hank taps the air with his pliers, pantomiming the mechanical Heimlich maneuver he'd just performed.

Jim thanks Hank and offers him a ten dollar bill. Hank nods his head and takes the money. I can see that they both feel like winners. Our generator runs, and a few minutes of easy work generated Hank a little gambling money.

Wow! First the man with the big compressor, just when we need him, and now the generator expert! And both in casino parking lots. Seems to be a good place to have emergencies. Of course, campers have always been known for their willingness to help their neighbors. We are living proof of that.

Doing the wash -- Camp style

39. Rural Luxury

As we stand listening to our generator, Alice, who is dressed in old jeans and a tank top today, but still wearing impossibly high-heeled sandals, tells me about a lovely rural campground nearby. Seems Hank works for a construction company and the couple lives in their little trailer while he moves from job to job. Until this weekend, they'd been staying in the park.

Alice goes on to explain that a Junior Olympics group booked all the spaces for this weekend months ago. "And so we had to move out," she says. "That's why we're camping here for the weekend." She points a be-ringed finger towards the casino and grins. "I don't mind."

They'll move back on Monday evening after Hank gets off work. "We couldn't stay here much more than a weekend," Hank grumbles with a tolerant smile for his wife. "We couldn't afford it!"

Monday morning, we hop into Froggy and go check out the park. We find that it is every bit as lovely as Alice had said, and nearly empty besides. The Junior Olympics group is gone and there's only one other space filled. As Alice has warned us, the park is somewhat primitive. They have water and electricity, and a communal dump station instead of individual sewer connections. There are no out-buildings. No office, no laundry, no showers, and no bathroom except for a couple of green PortaPotties. Nevertheless, it is much better than dry camping in gravel.

There is a camp host and so we knock on the door. A lady answers and explains that we have to pay for our space at the City Hall. She is only there to answer questions. We ask how much the sites cost and the price is $20, quite affordable. We go back to town, and stand in line behind a guy buying a license for his dog, a couple wanting marriage licenses and someone who wants to research a title. I laugh and observe to Jim, "Usually, when I stand in a line to get a campsite, the people ahead of me want things like laundry quarters, information, or something from the park store."

Our site paid for, we collect Rex and drive back to the campground. Before we install him into the tree shaded space we've chosen, we take advantage of their dump station to empty our holding tanks. Jim proudly shows me his latest find. Instead of the unpleasant job of rinsing the black water tank with a hose, he has discovered that Rex has a built in sprayer system. "See. You just attach the hose here." He points to where the hose connects to a valve on the black water tank. "And then, voila!" He turns the valve, and I can hear the water spraying inside the tank. We both stand there in admiration while Rex does the dirty work of rinsing out the tank.

Our chores done, we relax and enjoy the rural charm. We take a walk through the woods and I look for wildflowers to photograph. We stand by the creek and let flowing water mesmerize us. We sit at the picnic table with the sun warm on our backs and eat our lunch. The birds in the trees provide a pleasant musical background.

I wash out some undies and hang them on tree branches to dry. I think less kindly of the birds in the trees when I discover that one has left a big gray splotch on my just washed unmentionables. I rewash them and hang them out again . . . in a different, hopefully more protected place.

The pipes are up here

40. Water Willies

The next crisis comes on quietly. It starts with damp towels under the bathroom sink the same day we arrive at the park. Jim checks for leaks and doesn't find any. The area dries out and doesn't get wet again, even when we run water in the sink so we forget all about it. Then a few days later, I find wet towels again.

This time Jim has an answer. "I think it happens whenever I dump the black water tank," he says.

"Not sewage water!" I shriek.

"No, no, not sewage water. Remember that nifty little built-in spray system for cleaning the tank?"

"You think that's what it is?" I'm still not convinced.

"Yes," he assures me. "And if it is, the leak is water from pipes that are connected to fresh water."

I calm down and hope he is right.

He opens the bathroom cabinet door and points to the upper edge under the sink. "I see some pipes in there. I think they must transport the spray water." He pulls his head out of the cabinet. "I'll bet that's where the leak is," he says as he heads outside. "You watch while I turn on the spray," he directs.

"OK." Sounds easy enough. Then I realize that "watching" means that I must fit my not-so-thin self into the foot or so space between toilet and open sink cabinet. With effort, I manage to wedge myself in so that I can see the pipes—in fact, they are only a few inches away from my face. I pray that Jim is right; that it's "only water."

"It's on," Jim yells from outside.

"I know, I know," I squeal. "Turn it off!" I can see—and feel—the water squirting out of the pipe. Without a hand free to wipe my dripping face, I crawl out from my cramped quarters and, finally am able to scrub my face with a towel. It doesn't' smell. Jim was right—it isn't sewage water. I hadn't been completely sure . . . .

Another trip to a hardware store, a successful search for just the right part, and Jim soon has the problem fixed. This is the guy who, until he installed a new sink in my condo a couple of years ago, had never had any experience with plumbing! Since then, he's fixed toilets, put in a couple of showers and has now repaired Rex's spraying system. My husband, the handy man!

This nice park is where we decide to open our big awning for the first time. This should be a simple process. People do it all the time.

However, we really don't know what we are doing. Jim positions me at one side and himself at the other. Together we lift the heavy awning off its storage rack and try to set it up. Suddenly, I'm holding most of the weight of the awning and Jim's side is slipping to the ground. His bracket is broken and the awning itself is developing a rip.

We saw the awning rip, but who knows when the bracket broke. Like good second-hand buyers, we thought we'd checked everything. However, we missed the awning. We'll never know if we missed the damage then or if we did the damage ourselves just now.

We roll it back up. It fits almost as well as it did before and we leave it alone. Who needs an awning with all of these trees around anyway? We'll fix it later.

After five days in the park, we hit the road again, heading south. When we see a Camping World sign, Rex leaves the highway. I'm thinking that Jim has him trained to stop at every one!

Inside, Jim asks about a bracket for the awning. "Ah, yes, we have the part," the salesman says.

"Do you install?" I ask. Although I don't doubt Jim's ability to install it, I suspect it will involve climbing—something I'd just as soon avoid.

"Sure. That'd be, let's see," the man checks a chart, "$21 more."

Jim grins. We may be thrifty, but there are limits. For that price, he is glad to let them do the job. "Can you do it right away?" he asks.

"Sure," the salesman says. He disappears through a door behind the counter, supposedly to get the part. About the time we think he's forgotten us and gone to lunch, he returns. "Uh, we don't seem to have that part in stock after all," he reports. He brightens, "But we can order from Portland."

We'll soon be in Portland. Jim tells him to forget it. We'll get the part there. We've done without an awning so far; we can do without it a little longer.

41. Crab Lessons

At Olympia, we turn west, into the rain forests of Olympic Peninsula, where we have friends who live on a beautiful lake. They were one of the generous families who opened their homes to the homeless vagabonds we were last summer. This year, like a hermit crab, we bring our own home.

Dan and Marian invite us to park Rex on a concrete pad next to their house, built for just that purpose. However, Rex is too long. We'll have to find another place. We could stay at a casino—there are several on the peninsula. Instead, we choose a nearby RV park—it costs about the same as the one in Auburn and it is close to the lake.

We relax on Dan and Marian's big patio and watch the ever changing activity on the lake while we visit—speedy boats pulling water skiers or big rubber tubes filled with bouncing children, slower boats full of partiers, jet boats and more. The weather is perfect, warm with a breeze off the lake that keeps us comfortable. Towards evening, Dan suggests that we go out on the lake ourselves.

"You bet," we say.

Just the four of us, we rattle around in their big party boat, designed for ten or more. It's still hot, but the wind over the water and the occasional splash keeps us cool. This definitely beats hanging out in Rex, writing on my book and reviewing emails. But only for the day. We are still glad to have our own home on wheels to return to when the day is done.

Marian invites us to stay for dinner. "Do you like crab," she asks.

"You bet," we say—again. These guys know how to treat their guests right.

"Great! The store in Shelton had a sale on Dungeness crabs and I bought some."

At dinner, Marian serves up a whole crab to each of us. My fastidious husband stares in horror at the big, red-shelled, long-legged crustacean that covers his plate. It's easy to read his thoughts, "Oh, no, what do I do now? What have I gotten myself into?"

Jim doesn't enjoy eating messy food with his fingers, or as he says, "getting so intimately involved." He prefers a proper knife and fork. A good guest, he watches what we are doing and follows suit, manfully digging the meat out of his personal crab.

Dan, Marian and I dig and eat, dig and eat. Jim digs. And digs. And digs. Finally, with his shell empty and discarded, he cleans his fingers and eats his crab—with his fork.

A thrift queen's broken dream: No balls

42. Shoestring Sightseeing

After our visit with Dan and Marian we move Rex down to one of the casinos. We want to do some sightseeing and the casino is closer to where we will be. As thrifty travelers, we've learned to look for odd tourist attractions—the kind that are interesting, but seldom cost much. The book, *Weird and Wacky Washington Places,* by Bree Coven Brown and Lisa Wojna, and the internet, especially a website called *Roadside America* provide our information.

Our plan is to take Froggy on a 125 mile circle trip, towards the coast and then east to the I-5 corridor and west again on the same road we will travel tomorrow, on our way to Portland. A little less than 40 miles into our trip, we stop in Raymond, a town filled with, our book says, iron sculptures.

The sculptures are there, all over town, and just as fascinating as advertised. In fact, we find Raymond a budget sightseer's paradise with some of the better sculptures, a farmer's market and a couple of museums all in the same area. We take a closer look at the iron sculptures. Some are of people doing a variety of things. The one we like the best is flat, a horse in full leather harness, pulling a real buckboard wagon.

I want to take lots of photos—easy with my digital camera. That is, it would be easy if I hadn't left the memory card in the computer when I last transferred photos. We determine to come back again next year—with a working camera.

In the market, we find luscious fruit—and I promise myself we'll buy some of the big red, local strawberries before we leave. Further in, I stop at a table of linen tablecloths and runners done in cutwork embroidery. Jim likes the polished wood bowls. When I see handiwork, I usually look at it and think, "I could do that." But not here—the embroidery and the wood are both exquisite. A glance at Jim reminds me of our space restriction. I admire and amble on.

We really only have time—or energy—to visit one of the two museums in the complex. I give Jim his choice. He opts to bypass the one about carriages and chooses the seaport museum. Apparently, a vehicle must have a motor to be truly interesting.

As we walk on around the building towards the next museum, we see a woman relaxing, feet up on the bench, book in hand. When she spies us, she slams her book shut, jumps up from the bench and, with a big inviting grin, beckons to us.

"Oh, do come in," she bubbles, herding us into the building like a mother hen shepparding her chicks. We let her take charge, hardly knowing what's hit us. I look around for anything that gives a price. The energetic docent notices and explains, "Our museum is free, but we do accept donations at the end of your tour." Oh, yes, free is good. As for donations, we'll see . . . .

We are the only guests and she treats us like royalty. Eagerly, knowingly, the friendly lady begins her spiel, telling us about early life in Raymond—a seaport, and a logging town as well.

I'm entranced. My father and his brothers were all loggers in this same era. We go on with the tour, admiring the many dioramas that volunteer townspeople have built, using authentic items donated by local pioneers. Again, I wish for my camera. I promise myself that we'll come back next year and take lots of photos.

One display is of a variety of glass floats. I comment that I also collect these. "But, mine are stored—I don't have a place to display them anymore," I lament.

The docent almost jumps up and down, she's so excited "Oh, my! Would you like to sell them?" She too, collects these balls and unlike me, she has a place for hers—and wants more.

"I'm sorry, they're all back home in Arizona." I really am sorry—I think I might have sold them; they weren't doing me any good stored. Now, I'm really sorry that I let Jim talk me out of buying those that man was almost giving away in Wenatchee. The only thing better than a great bargain is selling it at great price!

As we leave, promising to return, Jim slips a $10 bill into the donation box. We may pinch pennies, but our tour, guided by this fascinating, well-informed woman, was worth it. Of course, I'd have been happier if, back in Wenatchee, Jim hadn't stopped me from loading Rex up with those bargain globes!

It's late afternoon by now, so we find a nice seafood restaurant—but we don't order crab. Even I have had my fill of crab for a while. We decide to postpone the circle trip. We can do it next year. I sleep most of the way home. I'm exhausted, a symptom, I know, of the lack of exercise our RV living brings. I guess we need to find more outlet malls.

43. Living in Storage

Before we left home I made arrangements to leave Rex in Dave's Storage Yard in Portland for the three weeks we will be gone. The yard is close to the airport and his ad promised airport transportation. It also is only a few miles from my son's home. It would be ideal if we could stay there in Rex for the week before and the week after we are in Alaska. I call Dave again and ask if this is possible.

"We usually don't let people live inside the yard, but I'll make an exception in your case," Dave tells us after some consideration. For a price, of course. The cost is still much less than that of an urban RV spot and so we are grateful. Thank you, Dave!

No one is about when we arrive and the gate sports a big rusty padlock. I use my cell phone to call Dave. His secretary answers and promises someone will be there to open the gate right away. I barely get my phone put away when a young man with dirty jeans and a rumpled shirt covering his skinny frame comes ambling out of an old trailer parked near the gate.

He introduces himself as Carl and says, "I'll have this gate open in just a minute." He accompanies his welcome with a smile that exposes several missing teeth, all on the same side of his mouth.

Carl struggle to find the right combination of key turns and twists to open the resistant padlock. While we watch, an older man arrives on a bicycle, a sack of supplies hanging from the handlebars. Oily gray hair curls onto a once-white T-shirt, but the big grin he directs towards us exposes a full mouth of teeth.

Finally, the lock clicks open and we drive through. The trailer door slams again and a young woman in equally grubby garb, joins us. "This is my fiancée, Lisa." Carl tells us. I struggle to hold back a startled giggle. Lisa's shy smile shows a mouth that is a twin to Carl's—the missing teeth are even on the same side.

I used to be an addictions counselor and detox nurse. Many of my clients had cocaine habits that had damaged their teeth and caused problems like Carl's and Lisa's twin smiles. I wonder about this couple; however right now, I'm more interested in simply settling into our new temporary home.

Carl invites us to park Rex just inside the gate and get out so he and Lisa can show us around. The old man follows us through, props his bicycle against the trailer, and joins our party. A man who obviously knows no strangers, he takes over as guide. As he shows us around, pointing out things of interest, we learn that his name is Homer and that he lives in the yard. Where in the yard, we never figure out. Surely not with Carl and Lisa; their little camper trailer is barely big enough for them. Homer tells us he works for tips. "I'm about ready to look for a real job," he adds. "Tips don't pay for much!"

Carl interrupts Homer's monologue to point out the many vehicles parked all over the storage yard. "I manage the yard," he says, with a quelling look at Homer—just in case we might think that the talkative Homer was in charge, I guess. "I can drive anything in here." Carl struts a bit and waves his hand to cover the whole yard full of a wide variety of large and small vehicles. Then, pointing to a spot between a big white delivery truck and an even bigger car-carrier trailer, he told Jim, "Here's where we are putting you. Just give me your keys and I'll back your rig in." Carl holds his hand out.

Jim keeps his keys in his pocket. 'No, that's fine. I can do it." I don't think he trusts Rex with someone who looks like a well-worn junkie.

Carl looks doubtful. He probably doesn't trust the old man to back in without damaging one or both the two rigs. Then he shrugs and Jim goes and gets Rex. With Carl directing, Jim deftly backs Rex into the narrow slot. Carl has the same look of bemused amazement on his face that my teenage grandsons had when Jim bested them at go-cart racing.

By the time we get settled, it's lunchtime. Jim turns on the generator so I can use the microwave to heat up some leftovers. We can run it all we want here. In a park, there's usually a curfew—no generators after 10 PM or before 7 or even 8 AM. But here, it is just one more noisy motor. Even at night, there's often a big motor running somewhere in the yard. I guess truckers aren't 9 to 5 guys, and a new vehicle is apt to arrive at any time. And when it does, it seems that often, Carl must move something around to make room for it.

With the airport so close, planes add to the noise by roaring over day and night. If we hear one when we're outside, Jim always looks up. I'll ask what it is and he can usually tell me. It is the same with cars. I don't know where he learns all of this.

Looking out from inside Rex

44. Keepers of the Gate

We are eating supper when Carl comes by to give Jim a key to the gate and a request. "Lisa and I are going to Dave's for dinner and a staff meeting." Carl struts a little, then looks exasperated. "Homer's gone. Can you let him in when he comes back? He'll be on his bike. Let him in, but don't let anyone else in." Hmm. They trust us, whom they've just met with a key, but not Homer?

"Did you notice the sack of groceries hanging from the handlebars of Homer's bike?" I ask Jim. "I don't think he's riding that bike just for his health," I said, speaking from my experience as an addiction counselor. Bikes and buses are often the main mode of transportation for people who have lost their driver's license due to drinking. Still, I give him credit for the bike. My most addicted clients tended to ignore a suspended license and drive anyway. "Homer isn't necessarily a practicing alcoholic, but I'll bet did more than his share of drinking in the past," I declare.

Jim and I play cards while we watch the gate. Homer doesn't show up, but a small dark blue car does. A woman gets out and rattles the gate. We play possum. She goes back to her car and honks the horn. We hide behind our drawn shades. She drives away but soon returns, followed by Carl who lets her in and leaves. She must have called Dave. The woman, whom we later learn is Dave's sister, drives over to a nearby storage container, opens it, and drags out furniture and boxes. Eventually, she drives away, leaving the door open and her belongings strewn about. The mess is still there when we leave a week later. It is summer, and the sun is shining—but this is Portland, and the rains WILL come, sooner, rather than later.

We return to playing cards. We are just putting them away when Homer finally arrives. Jim comes back from letting him in the gate saying, "He's not recovered yet. The fumes were almost enough to get me drunk." I doubt that he'll be finding a "real" job anytime soon. And in fact, we never see the man again. Dave may help out recovering addicts and alcoholics, but he apparently doesn't keep them around long if they *stop* recovering.

Sentry duty done, we go for a walk through the huge vehicle filled yard. We see more car carriers, some with wrecked cars on them, a variety of motorhomes and pleasure vehicles, few in good condition, large and small trucks, and lots of just plain junk. Dave has told us that he buys unclaimed storage bins. It looks like some of the less attractive stuff ends up here.

Towards the back of the yard, there's a huge pile of dirt. It's been there so long that the weeds growing on it are a foot high. A variety of small vehicles sit parked around it. "Wonder how that got here," I say to Jim. He just shakes his head. He isn't even going to guess.

We struggle around the edge of the pile of dirt, through brambles and around piles of junk to the edge of the lot where a slough runs.

I think of a slough (pronounced "slew") as a marshy creek, like the one that ran through our farm pasture when I was a kid. This is more like a canal, wide, deep and dark. Homer had promised us bird sightings and a mowed path beside the water. The path is there, mowed weeds, but we don't see any birds.

We do see large dark buildings on the other side of the water-way—a prison, according to Homer—and I find some Morning Glory. The photographer in me sees pretty white flowers with bright green meandering vines that will make a lovely photo. Farmers and road crews see them as tenacious weeds. We follow the path along the slough back to where Rex sits, separated from the mowed strip by a few brambles and a couple of old logs. Jim is sneezing. Our pastoral stroll has awakened his allergies.

The next morning, Jim stops for allergy pills before we drive Froggy over to visit my son Ken and get an internet fix. Ken and Deb are amazed that we'd stay in such a weird place as the storage yard. We try to explain the advantages—that it is close to them; that the price is right; that it is an adventure. I don't think they get it. Grown children can be so "inside-the-box."

The car carrier parked at the side of the road, before it became our neighbor.

45. Power, Power!

Experienced dry campers by now, we live quite comfortably. However, we do use our house batteries more when we dry camp. Bob warned us earlier about these old mismatched car batteries and the time has come to replace them. They no longer hold a charge overnight even when we have sun for our solar panel. That means we must do the "run the engine to charge the batteries to start the furnace" process like we did when it was raining. It's bad enough to think of dollars flying out the exhaust when we travel, but it is intolerable when we sit still.

I'm not looking for a bargain. Tired of having too little power, I insist on the best—and the heaviest, we learn. A kid, a football player from his size, packs our purchases out to our car, muscles bulging with the effort. We drive home and park in our usual space in front of Rex.

Oh, no. While we were gone, they moved a big black car carrier into the space next to Rex, with only about a foot between vehicles. The batteries fit in a basement (outside) compartment—naturally, on the side next to where the car carrier sits. We may have to wait to install them. And I was so looking forward to having more power! I take a closer look; I'm not ready to give up.

"Jim, look," I say. "If you move Rex forward a few feet so that the compartment door is past the car carrier's wheels, I think we can get it open." Then, pointing to the shoulder-high framework, I add, "And then you can stand under here to work."

Jim looks. Frowns. "Well, maybe."

I understand. He's the one who will work in this confined space. It is his back that will take the pressure of working stooped over. Still, he agrees to try, albeit hesitantly. He would like to have more power too and now that we have the batteries, he really doesn't want to wait anymore than I do.

But first, Jim and I must somehow get those huge blocks of lead out of the car trunk and over next to their new home. Jim backs Froggy as close to Rex as he can and still leave enough space for us to get the batteries out—the closer he can get to Rex now, the less we must move them later. With effort, we manage to lift the batteries out of the trunk and place them on the ground beside the Saturn. I'm wishing we'd bought the cheaper, lighter ones. Or better yet, that we'd brought along the kid with the bulging muscles.

After a short, but much-needed breathing spell, Jim moves the car forward again, leaving about a car-length between it and Rex. Next, I tuck myself into the space under the car carrier where Jim will eventually have to work and he drives Rex forward. Too bad I'm not the one who will be doing the work—I can actually stand. When Jim stops to let me try the compartment door I yell, "Six inches more." Jim creeps closer to the Saturn. "Six inches more," I yell again. And again. Rex's nose is almost touching the Saturn's trunk when, finally, I can lift the door and latch it open.

Jim now has plenty of space to work, except that he can't stand up without hitting his head on the carrier frame. He takes out the old batteries, checks the wiring and prepares the space for the new heavyweights. I prepare lunch—a cold one. We have absolutely no power since even the propane appliances need battery power to work. I call lunch and Jim happily crawls out to where he can straighten his back.

After lunch we move the batteries to the compartment. There's no way we are going to carry those big guys even a few feet. Instead, Jim and I drag them over and together, we lift them into the compartment. "Senior power" is when it takes two of us to do with great difficulty what Jim could once do easily alone.

The heavy lifting done, it doesn't take Jim long to get everything hooked up. Before he closes the door, he comes in and checks the fridge. Its lights are on. He turns on the house lights and they work. He digs out a lamp and plugs it in the inverter socket and flips the switch. It shines! We have power! Hurrah!

This evening, we celebrate by watching one of our thrift shop VCR tapes and then about ten or so, I go to bed. I'm not asleep yet when Carl knocks on our door. They are moving the car carrier out. He needs to move Froggy from its regular space in front of Rex so they will have maneuvering room. Right. *Now*, they move the car carrier.

In the morning, we run our furnace without having to recharge the batteries even though we used the TV and VCR last night. What a treat!

46. Clean up day

Tomorrow we leave for Alaska. That makes today "clean-up, eat-up" day. We do our best to finish everything that is in the fridge. What we can't use I'll give to my friend Sally, who is meeting us for lunch. The road to her home connects with I-5 only a few miles from a roadside rest area with a dump station. It is the closest free one we've found, so we are taking Rex there this morning. We justify the extra miles we are driving to avoid a hefty dumping fee by agreeing that we both enjoy Sally and will be glad to visit with her.

So that we can move Rex, Jim transfers Froggy into the place where the carrier used to sit. I ask if he thinks this is wise. "There's never anything there during the day anymore," he replies. True. A small cable-installing company has been using the space as a company garage for their fleet of white trucks and vans. We hear the drivers arrive, talking Spanish, early in the morning and watch them return every day around five. We plan to be back well before then.

It's about eleven when we head out, sitting high and looking down on the world—a big change from the perspective in the little Saturn, our transportation for the last week. Soon we are crossing the bridge between Oregon and Washington. Traffic is light and it takes us less than a half-hour to drive the 25 miles up I-5 to the rest area.

After we dump, Jim pulls forward to the clean water so he can fill the water tank. There's no faucet handle. Instead there's this big red button. Jim gives it a push. He guessed right; the water turns on. It runs for a few seconds and then it stops. Puzzled, Jim pushes the button again. Water gushes out, but again, it stops. Finally, Jim looks at the little sign posted below the button. Ah, yes ". . . automatic shut-off in 40 seconds . . ." he reads out loud to me.

"I guess someone let the water run over," he mutters. Or maybe several "someones," I think. With a sigh, Jim patiently stands there and pushes the red button every 40 seconds over and over until the water fills our eighty gallon tank.

One of the drawbacks of dry camping is the limited water supply coupled with a limited holding space. To combat this at least once, Jim plans to stay in the rest area to shower. "We can use all the water we want and when we are done, we can dump and fill again."

Thinking ahead, he adds, "And we can store Rex ready to use when we return." I am all for that. Then, we shouldn't have to move Rex out of the storage yard again until we are ready to move on. That's good because moving Rex out of the yard can be a major project—moving the Saturn out of the way is the least of it. We never know if Carl will park other vehicles in our way. Of course, there's the careful backing up, often between two large vehicles. Finally, the way things change in the yard, there's the fear that Carl will fill our parking spot with another vehicle while we are gone. Yes, we want to move Rex as little as possible.

Now we discover that Jim's showering plan won't work. We can't stay where we are; there's a line of RVs behind us. We can't pull back into the rest area; the turn is too sharp. Jim moves to Plan B. "No problem," he says with a grin. "I'll just cross the freeway and we can stop in southbound rest area." Of course, that entails a drive north for several miles to the next bridge across the freeway and then back. Oh, well it's a nice day for a drive.

After a short "scenic tour" we return, this time on the south side of I-5. I win the draw and get to go first. I'm looking forward to cleaning up. Due to my aversion to Rex's shower—I haven't had more than a spit bath for a week. Although Jim hasn't said anything, he is likely looking forward to a cleaner housemate too.

Even now, my shower can't be leisurely. While I can use all the water I want, Rex's water heater limits me to six gallons. The water is running cool by the time I rinse my hair. Feeling cleaner than I have in ages, I towel off and don clean clothes. Ahh! I grab a bottle of water and we play a game of cards while we give the water heater time to provide hot water for Jim.

While he showers, I empty the fridge and package up our unused perishables for Sally. I save out only enough sandwich supplies to make us a lunch for the flight to Anchorage. That way we won't have to buy one of those airplane box lunches that have replaced the free meals we used to complain about and now wish we still got.

Once Jim is dressed, it is dump time again. And push-the-red-button-every-40-seconds fill-up time again. Jim has me keep my foot on the toilet flusher so it runs water into the black tank—we have another day to live in Rex before he is stored and it is better to have very watery sludge than dry sludge. The foot-operated toilet flusher is about a foot off the floor and at the best of times, not easy for me to operate. By the time Jim is satisfied that we have enough water, my leg has started to cramp. I suspect his thumb is equally sore from all of that button pushing.

As expected, we enjoy our visit with Sally, one of my favorite people, with her curly red hair and always interesting stories. She's a part-time widow. Her husband works at a job that keeps him away so much that in all the years I've known her, I've only met him once. While he's gone, Sally likes to buy and renovate homes. Her most recent project is located half-way up a mountain. We visited her aerie—once. Our trip, with 15 miles of switchbacks, deep chasms and breathtaking views made me realize how different we are. For me, visiting such a place is an adventure; living there would be . . . drudgery. For her it is a wonderful hideaway.

Sally is always excited about something. Besides being an excellent carpenter, she's also a great artist, photographer and budding writer. We spend our lunch updating her on our travels, listening to her latest adventures with her house—she's renovating a bathroom. She regales us with stories about the wildlife that lives near her mountain home—a deer family, some coyotes, lots of birds. We finish lunch and are just saying our goodbyes when my cell phone rings.

It is Carl at the storage yard. They want to put a large truck where Jim parked the Saturn. The restaurant is 20 miles from the yard, so I give them an ETA of about a half an hour—longer than it took us to get to the rest area, which was further away. However, it is nearly 3 pm. Rain, early rush hour traffic and a collision we eventually manage to pass slows us down. Forty-seven tense minutes later, we drive in through a wide open gate and past a huge flatbed truck parked just inside, motor running.

Jim backs Rex into his space and moves the Saturn out of the way. With an impatient rev of its motor, the truck takes up residence where Froggy had been. So much for Jim's theory of "there's never anything there during the day." Few routines continue unchanged for long in the storage yard. The cable company crews return at the usual time, but today, they park in a different place.

We spend our evening playing cards as we often do. I begin to feel chilly, but instead of donning a sweater, I turn the furnace on for the first time in days. "As much as anything, to see if it still runs," I say. Soon I'm far too hot and the sweater comes off. Shades of menopause. I quit playing cards and go to bed, leaving Jim to enjoy the heat from the furnace.

It's travel day and Jim is up early, doing his usual stirring around in the kitchen. I hear him trying to light the stove. Click, click. Pause. Click, mutter. Uh-oh, I'll bet the fire starter has run out of fluid. I know it is low. I think we have a spare. It should be there somewhere, but I know that man-like, Jim is useless at finding things. I roll out and stumble into the kitchen, where Jim greets me with, "We have no propane."

Oh, no. We focused so on our dumping trip yesterday that we forgot to get propane while we had Rex out. Neither one of us even thought to check its level. Oh, well, it's too late now. It is almost time to leave for the airport. We'll have to take Rex out for propane as soon as we return—just what we were trying to prevent.

In the meantime, Jim starts the generator. With microwave, toaster and coffee pot, we do fine for breakfast. However, we freeze, because of course there is no furnace and no stovetop burners. I remember how I ran the furnace last night "just to see if it worked" and how over-heated I had been. I wish I'd waited for this morning to give it that test. I sure could use some of that warmth now!

Over Snow Covered Mountains

47. Up in the Air

Our flight leaves at noon and transportation to the airport on the day of departure was included in our rental agreement with Dave. However, it's a quarter to ten and no transportation has appeared, nor is there any activity around Carl's trailer. I call Dave's office and his secretary says, "Oh, yes, that's ten PM, right?"

Alarmed, I reply, "No, ten AM."

"I'll call over there," she promises.

I go outside and amble towards the gate, hoping to see some activity. Sure enough, the door of the manager's trailer flies open and Lisa comes bounding out, hair uncombed. "We'll go in my car," she tells me pointing to a dirty little once-green Chevy. Well, Dave promised transportation. He didn't promise luxury—or even clean for that matter.

Jim and Lisa are cramming our bags into the Chevy's small trunk when Carl comes out. I ask if he'd got the wrong message and thought we left in the evening.

"No, I knew it was this morning." He apologizes for oversleeping and talks about working well into the night, moving vehicles around. I believe him. I heard the motors running, but that's become a part of living in a storage yard.

Jim joins us now, keys in hand. "Here are keys to both vehicles and the gate key you loaned us too," he says to Carl. Jim trusts Carl with Rex now, after watching him move so many large vehicles around.

"Oh yes. I almost forgot about keys. Without them, we'd really be in a fix if we need to move one of your vehicles." Knowing how things in the yard move around, I fully expect to find Rex in a new spot when we return.

We squeeze ourselves into the back seat of the two-door vehicle— Lisa's belongings litter the front—and head for the airport only a little late. For once check-in goes quickly and we find we now have an hour and a half to kill. On a trip to the ladies room, I discover a "Service Center," a room with desks, plug-ins, and free Wi-Fi. What a treat for us computer guys! Now we wish we'd asked for an eight AM delivery time ten, but it's probably just as well. Carl and Lisa needed their sleep.

On the plane we eat the lunch I packed and drink their free drinks. "I wonder when they will begin to charge even for the soft drinks," I comment. Jim shrugs and drags out his computer.

As Jim reads the email he has downloaded and I read my book, we fly high over ocean and snow capped mountains to Fairbanks, Alaska where my daughter, Sue and her family live.

My Fairbanks Office

48. Trading Spaces

In Fairbanks, we temporarily trade our life in Rex with his continual crises, but also his queen-size bed and our own living and work spaces for the top floor of my daughter's home with its double bed and a recreation room we share with the great-grandkids' toys.

We are grateful that Sue banished the kids themselves from the whole second floor while we are there. Although we enjoy the young ones in small doses, it is a blessing to be able to escape up the stairs when our age begins to show.

Of course, there are drawbacks. Sue's house isn't set up for Wi-Fi and her computer is downstairs. The thought of going without an internet connection of our own for three weeks is unacceptable. When Jim discovers that his favorite store has an outlet even in distant Fairbanks, we head off to the world's most northern Walmart. He finds a wireless router, and back at Sue's, quickly gets it hooked up. The whole house, including our upstairs quarters, is now wired for Wi-Fi. Aged we may be, but where computers are concerned, we rule! And a new router is small pay for the luxury of a whole floor to ourselves—even if it does lack a bit in furnishings.

Our next project is to set up an office. Jim's email traffic never stops and I'm writing an article on Lewy body dementia for an Alzheimer's newsletter. I glance around our new home space. It doesn't look promising. There are two bedrooms with the usual bed and dresser, a workout room crammed with gym equipment that doesn't get much use and a bathroom with a tub. A tub! I haven't had a bath since we left Mesa. The promise of a real bath after my experiences with showers for the last month almost takes my mind off the job of setting up our office.

Pulling myself back to my task, I spy a couple of folding TV trays and two folding chairs. I set these up in the free space left in the middle of the room, and we are in business.

Ta-da!

49. Playing Tourist

It isn't all work. After all, we are in Alaska and we do want to play tourist some of the time. Sue loans us their little purple Subaru Baja for transportation. Like always, Jim drives. We do the usual stuff like pan for gold and tour the downtown Ice Museum. Sue gives us an over night trip to Chena Hot Springs that she won at a local auction. We find the tour of the novel geothermal plant that heats the whole place and cools their little ice museum as well a highlight of our trip.

The Hot Springs also sports an indoor swimming pool, several hot tubs and a huge pond, called Rock Lake. We skip the kid-filled indoor pool and go outside, where we climb into an adults-only tub. There we meet Suzanne and Arthur, from New York by way of Florida, their present home base. Passionate RVers, they drove their motorhome up the Alcan. While we lounge in the almost too hot water, Suzanne tells me, "My friends were surprised that I liked motor-homing. They thought I'd motor to the closest five-star hotel and check in." She adds, "We don't eat out anymore either, so we save more money than we spend on gas and we are healthier."

Jim and I look at each other, but don't say anything. We probably eat out more when we are RVing than when we aren't. I remember the couple with the big diesel pusher in the casino parking lot who were so thrifty and I think again that maybe that's how the rich stay rich, and mentally shrug. Not for me. I LIKE eating out now and then. But then, Rex is paid for. That's the beauty of having an older RV.

We all move to the hot-springs-fed Rock Lake, a large man-made pond surrounded by huge rocks and aerated by a tall spray of water in the center. Ouch! It's even hotter than the hot tub. However, by cooling off occasionally under the icy-cold spray, I manage to stay for a while. I want to visit more with these interesting people who, like us, spend months at a time in a small wheeled space and think they are living it up.

While the guys visit, Suzanne asks me about what they should see in Alaska. I suggested the pipeline viewing station near Fairbanks as one option. When I was there, I found the equipment on display especially fascinating. "You will find out that a retired pig isn't your husband," I joke, referring one of the displays. Arthur smiles weakly and makes some comment about how their way of motoring doesn't use a lot of gas. It isn't until later that I realize that he thought I was calling him a gas hog! I hope they do go to the viewing station and discover that a "pig" is a huge piece of equipment that travels inside the four-foot diameter pipeline, a mechanical pipe cleaner. And of course, the one on display is "retired."

50. A Dinner Out

Since our stay is paid for, we splurge our own money on a nice dinner in the rustic restaurant. The window by our table looks out on a bird feeder—watched over by a proprietary squirrel. Ivan, a Russian student in Fairbanks earning money over the summer, waits on us. He tells us that at first, the squirrel wouldn't allow any birds there at all. "Now," Ivan says in excellent English, "he's given up the fight, and only chases them off if they get into the middle of the feeder."

I pull out my ever-present camera and take some photos. Something about that black box sets the squirrel off. Maybe he thinks the camera is hungry and about to encroach on his territory. The furious rodent rushes up to the window and started scolding, "Churrrr, Churrr, Churrr." With my help, the chastised camera retreats back into its case. His challenge successful, the squirrel goes back to eating.

**Anyone could use the top lever
for the gear shift, right?**

51. Not Another Rex!

Jim and Randy go off somewhere to do guy stuff. Sue and I had planned to have a good gabfest when she remembers her hair appointment. "I have to go, Mom," she wails. "I've had this appointment with Sandi for six months and if I don't go, she'll likely make me wait months and months before I can get in again—if ever."

I must have looked a bit surprised. I was. I couldn't imagine my hairdresser refusing to see me because I cancelled an appointment. After all, it was just a $10 haircut. For me, that is. Sue pays a bit— well, a lot more, I'm sure. Still . . . .

Seeing my confused look, Sue explains, "Nobody misses an appointment with Sandi. Not if you want to stay in her good graces. Even if you cancel a few days early, she puts you at the end of her three month-long waiting list.

I must still look skeptical, so Sue continues, "Let me tell you what happened when my doctor and his wife, Jackie, went to Hawaii for a month. About halfway through their stay, Jackie remembered she had a hair appointment with Sandi coming up. Jackie insisted they come home right away so she wouldn't miss it." Sue shrugged, "I'd have done the same thing. You just can't afford to miss an appointment with Sandi."

Maybe it's the difference between still working at a high paying job and being retired and on a limited income. I suspect I could find a place even in isolated Fairbanks—a cheaper place, a bargain place, where they would welcome my business and wouldn't think of instilling such fear about a canceled appointment.

However, to my frantic daughter, I say, "Go! I'll be fine here. Maybe I'll take the Subaru and go check out the Goodwill store— or that used bookstore I found the last time I visited." These are things better done alone. Sue likes a bargain, but she isn't into them like I am.

I use the quiet to finish my article and email it to Jim's computer for a final review. That didn't take long, so now, I'm ready to go shopping. I grab the keys and climb into the little purple car.

Although I've not yet driven the Subaru, it has an automatic transmission, so it shouldn't be that difficult. The car starts, but when I try to shift, it just won't move. What? Another Rex? The blamed thing works for Jim. Why not for me? Over and over, I try. No luck. I am stomping back into the house with tears of anger and frustration streaming down my face when Sue returns.

"Your blasted car won't work," I tell her.

"Can you show me?" she asks since we are still standing outside.

I climb back in, turn the key and try to shift.

Sue bends over laughing. Eventually she stops long enough to gasp, "Mom, you're trying to shift with the windshield wipers! Didn't you see them going back and forth?"

No, I hadn't. I was trying to back up after all. Besides, I'd pushed the control all the way to intermittent. I'll never live this down.

A mud puddle on a hot day: Hog Heaven

52. Walking the Pigs

Today, we are going to learn about walking pigs. Yes, pigs. Christian, Sue and Randy's 13 year-old grandson, is raising them as his 4-H project.

"You have to walk your pigs?" I ask. When Sue was a baby, we raised pigs on our own small farm, but ours never left the pen. Well, it was a big pen, but still . . . .

"Yes, at least a mile every day so they develop muscle instead of fat." Apparently weight isn't enough. It has to be the right kind of weight. Things have changed since my pig-farming days.

"Would you like to come with us, Grandma Helen?"

I would. What's good for the pigs should also be good for me. Out of curiosity, urbanite Jim agrees to go too. He's never seen a pig, except for those safely penned at a fair. Besides, I'm not the only one who hasn't been getting enough exercise.

Christian is part of Sue's large extended Fairbanks family. He and his parents and siblings live between two sets of grandparents. In a semi-rural setting, Sue and Randy's home sits on the edge of an acre of yard. The other set of grandparents own a gentleman's farm nearby. Family members who live further away visit often. As usual, Jim's head spins as he tries to figure out who is who and how they are all connected. At least the relationships aren't as convoluted as mine—no cousins marrying sisters.

Christian keeps his pigs in a pen at the farm, so that's where we start. Walking the pigs is a family activity. Christian, his mom and Grandma Sue herd the three pigs. Christian's siblings come because they are too young to leave alone. Six-year-old Caleb drives a miniature four-wheeler and five-year-old Larissa drives a child-sized pink electric jeep with its radio set permanently on high. Jim and I tag along for the exercise. Randy is working and the other grandparents are out of town, or they might have joined us too.

With the radio for a marching band, all we need are flags. Our trek takes us along gravel roads bordered by average sized homes in huge yards—land is cheaper than lumber here. When we turn onto a two-lane paved road, people drive by gawking. Some stop to ask what's going on. A moose wouldn't have surprised them; but a parade of pigs and kids?

The pigs run loose, their herders prodding them along with canes. A tap on the heel sends them forward. A tap on a cheek moves them sideways. It's hot, in the 90's, so we stop at a big mud puddle and let the pigs cool off. A pig lolling in a puddle on hot day is a picture of ultimate bliss.

Yesterday, it rained, thus the presence of puddles. That's when the pigs like to root in the neighbors' nice damp lawns. Since this is not as acceptable as puddle-lolling, Christian works to keep his charges on the road—and himself in his neighbors' good graces. His labor pays off. At the end of summer, long after we are gone, he wins Reserve Champion with one of his pigs at the State Fair.

53. The Pied Piper of Fairbanks

Christian's little brother Caleb is also in the livestock business, raising 4-H turkeys. He and his family take off on a two day trip, leaving us to care for the animals in their absence. After we go to the farm and help Sue walk Christian's pigs, Jim and I go over to Caleb's house to deal with the turkeys. Same thing—they too, need to be in good shape for the fair. When the family is home, they let the turkeys out to roam around the yard during the day.

"But won't they run off?" I asked Caleb earlier.

"No way, grandma," Caleb told me with six-year-old authority. "Turkeys are like other birds. They have a territory and they stay in it."

Turkeys are typical birds in another way too. I learn quickly to watch where I walk.

With no one home, the flock of three crowd together in a small pen and therefore, need to be walked as well as fed. When Jim opens the gate, the almost fully grown white turkeys strut through, taking their time and checking things out. Then, suddenly seeming to realize they are free, they lose their dignity, flap their wings and run to the house. Oh, yes, food. They have their heads in the pan before we get the pellets poured out of the bag.

We check the water in their pen and decide they should have more. This involves filling up a bucket from a spigot near the house and carrying it through grass and debris to their gate, then carefully into the pen. I stay by the faucet near the house and do the filling. My fastidious husband manfully does the heavy toting, carrying the buckets through grass and debris to the pen and then over the messy, turkey-poop covered floor to the water bowl at the back.

By the time we finish with the water, the turkeys have cleaned up all their food and need to be walked. This entails simply walking around and encouraging the turkeys follow. I take a turn while Jim carefully cleans his shoes and they follow—sort of. Then Jim takes over and all three birds fall right into line. Apparently, they like Jim a lot better than they do me. Maybe his long legs are easier to follow. Jim doesn't mind. It's a much simpler job than walking the pigs.

I watch while Jim plays Pied Piper, leading the turkeys around the yard. The tom, tail out in a handsome spread takes the back position. The two young hens, flapping their wings and squawking in their efforts to keep up with long legged Jim, dance along in the middle. Another parade—with no one to see it except me—and my camera.

When the ice isn't thick enough....

54. Land of the Midnight Sun

It's time to catch the red-eye back to Portland. With everything an hour or more behind the rest of the nation, these middle-of-the-night flights are the most common way for Alaskans to leave the state. The flights are also cheaper, which of course, makes them attractive to me. They are attractive in another way too; you can sleep on the plane and arrive in early morning, ready to face the day. At least, that's the plan. The last time I took this flight, I sat between my not-small husband and a bearded giant of a man who played action games on his computer for the whole trip. I didn't get much sleep—but I did learn how to play Myst.

Although I'm usually in bed by ten, we both stay up tonight, getting packed and saying our final goodbyes. Since Sue and Randy both must work tomorrow, they are taking us to the airport around eleven although our flight doesn't leave until one.

The airport is little more than a stone's throw away. However, the Chena River flows across the stone's path. We must drive five miles east to a bridge, then back again for another five miles.

"It only takes me five minutes in winter," Sue brags.

"How's that?" Jim asks. He's the chechacko—the newcomer. He's still learning about Alaska.

"I just drive the ice road across the river," she explains. Five minutes and a certain amount of courage—or well, some consider it stupidity. Once the ice is firm enough to tolerate a vehicle, it's possible to be at the airport well before the inside of the car is warm.

The challenge is to know when it's safe. Too early in the fall or too late in the spring, and you, your passengers and your car all take a dip in freezing waters. Sometimes, right in the middle of winter, Fairbanks temperatures can spike for several days from their usual single-digit temperatures to a balmy forty or so even in winter. This makes the ice mushy—and unsafe.

Of course, the ice road isn't an option now and I'm glad. Guess I'm not as brave as my daughter, and especially not in the middle of the night. Not that it is dark. In fact, as we cross the bridge and turn back towards the airport, Sue reaches into box between the front seats and comes out with sunglasses. The sun, now sitting on the horizon, is so bright that Sue needs them to be able to see. Shades at 11 pm. Right! Nevertheless, I wish I had some too.

At the airport, we find going through security a much simpler task in Fairbanks than it was in Portland—and much faster. However, this small airport doesn't provide amenities like Wi-Fi. We people watch, nap a bit and read until plane time. Again, it is an uneventful flight.

55. Back In Storage

Ken meets us and, good son that he is, takes us out for breakfast before delivering us to the storage yard. This time we travel in style, in Deb's roomy—and clean—Camaro, a far cry from Lisa's crowded and dirty little utility car.

We spend an hour or so catching up on family and sharing our adventures in Alaska with Ken. Not that Alaskan adventures are new to my son. He lived and worked there for years. Like many Alaskans, he had a well-paid job that came with a heavy traveling schedule. He quit and moved to Portland when Deb gave him an ultimatum: his family or his job. She was tired of being a single parent. The pay isn't as good now, but Deb is happier—and Ken admits that he is too. A family man at heart, he isn't sorry he made the change.

At the restaurant, I use my cell phone to call Dave's office and to let them know we will soon arrive at the storage yard. The secretary promises to let Lisa and Carl know we are coming. Sure enough, a short honk when we arrive at the gate brings Lisa running to let us in. Working a new combination lock, she has the gate open in half the time it usually takes Jim. We drive through and I get out to collect our keys.

"Oh, of course!, she exclaims when I ask for them. She dashes back and grabs a locked box from just inside the door. While we watch, she unlocks it and exposes a tangled rat's nest of at least a hundred keys. As she paws through the contents, my awe turns to apprehension. How will she know which are ours?

"I know they're here somewhere," she insists. Yeah, sure. Somewhere. I begin thinking about how to break into Rex.

"Here they are!" she shouts as she and pulls out a tag with our keys attached. Whew! She hands them over along with a key to the same contrary lock Jim used before to open the gate. Guess Jim doesn't get to use the new combination one.

We find Rex and Froggy in fine condition. Nothing's missing or out of place. No big trucks have backed into them. No one's taken them joy riding—well, they are in a different spot, but we expected that.

Portland is having a rare heat wave. Even this early in the day, it's getting hot in our tin box. Rex's insulation is limited. Ken told us that it's supposed to be in the high nineties all week—with humidity to match. We turn on the AC, glad it doesn't run on propane—which Jim reminds me, we need to get. It may be hot now, but it will get chilly when the sun goes down, and then we'll want the furnace. We also need propane for the refrigerator, which isn't running either. Yes, we definitely need to get propane.

We find the location of the nearest source from Carl. Then, because Jim hates surprises when he is driving the cumbersome RV, we go there in Froggy first. We need groceries anyway.

We got to Walmart and pick up some things and then stop at a produce stand. Due to the need for shipping, produce in Alaska tends to be as expensive as the quality is poor. Therefore, like most Alaskans, when I'm turned lose in a produce store "outside," I go wild. Even after all these years of living out of the state, I tend to buy far too much. This time is no exception.

The still-non running fridge now stuffed with fruit and veggies, we take Rex to get his propane fix. After Jim pays for the propane—and starts the fridge, he suggests, "Let's go gas up Rex while we have him out."

"Good idea," I agree. Gas is always a few cents cheaper at Costco. The way Rex guzzles gas, a few cents per gallon adds up. It means we'll have to drive to their closest store, about five miles away. However, a short side trip now when we aren't in a hurry will be one less thing we have to do when we leave.

By the time we arrive, it's past one o'clock. After our busy morning, we're both hungry. Usually, we'd eat out at Jim's favorite restaurant, the food service court just inside Costco. However, we have all that nice fresh produce I just bought, so I decide we'll "eat in." While Jim is out watching the numbers spin on the gas pump, I fix lunch.

I've just dumped a can of tuna into my salad when Jim comes in with the receipt—the usual $99. "Did you fill the tank?" I ask although I knew what his answer would be. Jim shakes his head. I smile. I'd guessed right. It usually takes more than the amount the pumps allow us to charge at one time. He seldom bothers to run the cycle again. Or maybe he can't tolerate doing it again . . . .

I set out our silver. "Lunch is ready."

"OK, but I need to move over into the parking lot first." I guess he should. We are still in front of the pumps. The cars behind us will be honking if we don't!

Settled in an out-of-way spot at the edge of the Costco parking lot, we sit down to eat. Relaxed and enjoying the experience of being in our own home again, we take our time, reminiscing about this and that. When we finish our salad, I clear the table and Jim brings out the cards. I'm winning my second game—an exciting and unusual event for me—when I glance out the window and see all the parked cars. For a moment, I'm confused and then I realize where we are. "Uh, we should probably leave," I say.

"Huh?" Jim has been as oblivious of our surroundings as I have. He looks around. "Oh, yeah, I guess we should. We've been here a while." He looks at his watch. "A couple of hours in fact." The joy of RVing is that you can be as at home in a Costco parking lot as you are in a fancy resort park.

56. Tow Truck Delivery

The next day we go over to Ken's to check our mail, get our internet fix and visit a bit with the kids—well, kids to us—my son and his wife are both in their late forties. Our teenage grandson, Brandon is there—an unusual occurrence since he is usually out with his friends or working at his summer job at the paint ball park. We spend some time with him and he invites us to come play paint ball. Uh, no, thanks. However, we enjoy our visit. These kids grow up too soon!

Back at the gate, Jim is doing his usual patient fumbling with the padlock when a fellow gets out of a shiny green SUV parked outside the fence and comes over. He introduces himself as Bob and explains that like we did, he's arranged to leave his car here and get a ride to the airport. He's been waiting for about 15 minutes and he's getting worried. No one appears to be around. "Did you honk?" Jim asks.

"Yeah, and I even yelled. No one answered."

Jim explains that we are just guests. "Call Dave again," he suggests. "There's always someone at the office." We could have been Good Samaritans and taken Bob to the airport, but we couldn't do anything about storing his car, so we go on in and leave him to deal with his dilemma.

No more than a few minutes later, we hear a big motor. A tow truck comes roaring up and Lisa jumps out. She opens the gate and ushers Bob into the yard. He parks where she indicates and climbs out of his SUV, briefcase in hand. He's shuffling his feet and looking around. My guess is he's looking for the car that is supposed to transport him to the airport.

Lisa hops out, dashes around to the other side of the truck and opens the passenger door. She stands back and with a flourish, invites Bob to get in. I can see his mouth open in surprise. He says something, and Lisa shakes her head and points again to the passenger seat. With a glance at his watch and a shrug, he tosses his brief case in and follows with an undignified but successful scramble. That first step must be at least two feet off the ground.

Jim and I look at each other in amazement as the truck rumbles away. She's taking him to the airport in a tow truck! We are back in the storage yard, where things are never the same, yet always interesting.

We develop a routine. Work around the motorhome until noon or so and then leave for places with air conditioning, returning in early evening. Yes, our roof-top air conditioner works just fine. However, it takes gas to run, so it's expensive. Besides, it is as old as Rex. Who knows when IT will decide to quit. We use it as needed but we are grateful for other resources.

Carl and Lisa aren't around as much this time. We do talk to them occasionally. We already know that their boss is an inveterate entrepreneur, starting up new businesses regularly. They tell us that Dave's latest new business is an indoor storage place a few blocks away. He's renovating the building and has the couple working over there most of the time.

Carl brags, "Dave says if we help out now, he'll let me manage the store. And I'll get a share of the profits."

Apparently, they are presently working only for barter. I'm not sure what they get besides a place to live—but I don't think it's money.

"We have bills," Lisa complains.

"But Dave says that if we take a salary, he won't set us up in business." Carl, the dreamer, is for holding out for the big time.

Lisa, the realist, mumbles, "I'd rather have a salary."

During this final week in my old stomping grounds, I make time to visit old friends one more time, do some shopping in familiar stores and simply enjoy the lush green scenery. As usual, when I am enjoying the weather, Jim is sniffling. He's becomes a steady customer of allergy drugs—which help a little, but definitely don't stop his sniffles altogether.

We usually start our day at Ken's, visiting and checking our email and once, washing our clothes. Sometimes no one is home, but we know how to get in. Then, besides visiting friends and shopping, we do some exploring. We visited the Portland Rose Garden—a beautiful place with umpteen varieties of roses, most of them in bloom. Jim enjoys the flowers—as he pops another allergy pill. Another time, we float up the Willamette River on a big stern-wheeler. We value this lazy relaxed time because we know we'll be back on the road again very soon.

57. RV Time Shares

We finally get around to checking with the Portland Camping World about the awning part—the part that the people in Tacoma said they could order from the Portland store. We discover that we've procrastinated too long. Now, they don't have the part either. Of course, they too are willing to order it, but can't promise it will arrive before we leave. Oh, well, the summer is almost over and we've done just fine without an awning so far. We solve this problem like we did the air conditioning and the transmission problems. We let it go, at least until next year.

While we are at Camping World, a friendly young man comes up and invites us to learn about his RV campground program. We've been thinking about doing something like this so we let him usher us into his web, uh, office. Buying a campground membership is a lot like buying a time share. You have a home park at which you can camp for free for a certain number of nights a year. And then, there are many other parks that you can pay a minimal fee to use.

Of course, a membership's initial cost can be $5,000 to $10,000 and then there are the yearly dues which can add up to more than $500 a year. We are not about to pay that much.

However, it is the end of the summer. The economy is on the skids and gas is way too high. Our salesman is hungry and willing to make a great deal. He finally makes an offer we like. For well under $1000 we have a limited membership—all we need. Since we won't be using the membership this year, they also waive the first year's dues. Ah, yes! We are now Real RVers. We overnighted in a Walmart parking lot, drove miles our of our way for gas and now, with Happy Camper and this one, finally have two RV park memberships. We look forward to an easy life of full hookups, cable TV, Wi-Fi and lots of activities next year.

Of course, it might not be as adventurous as it has been this year. Thinking back, we've stayed in a truck stop, Walmart parking lots, casinos, a church yard, a beauty shop parking lot, this storage yard and even a few RV parks. Our boondocking, while not over, will be much less. Like a couple looking back on their early penny-pinching youth, I suspect we will remember our first year of RVing with nostalgia. Although I doubt that we'll want to relive the adventures we've had this year, I'm sure we will enjoy the memories.

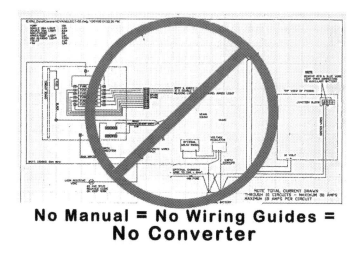

No Manual = No Wiring Guides = No Converter

58. Mixed up Wiring

I've asked my electrician son to come check out Rex's funny wiring. I hope that he can fix whatever it is that prevents the generator or park power from charging our batteries. When clouds or rain limit the solar panel's effectiveness, our batteries, even the new ones, lose much of their charge. Luckily, the engine WILL recharge them. However, I hate having to run the engine for such a purpose, especially in a park with "piped in" electricity.

Jim is lukewarm about this project; with better batteries, he believes we can get the power we need from the solar panel. I want more. I want what most RVers have: the ability to charge Rex's batteries from generator or park power as well.

For most of our light, we use lamps that we plug into the AC outlets. These take much less than the DC lights. I would prefer to use the centrally-located house lights built into the RV.

"But the lights are DC, so they only run with battery power," Jim explains.

I know. Before I met Jim, I spent several winters in an old Holiday Rambler travel trailer in an Arizona RV park. Park electricity channeled through a converter charged the batteries and kept the lights working well—as long as the converter did its job. However, it kept burning out and I went through three before the repairman finally fixed the problem. By then, I'd learned more than I ever wanted to know about converters and how they work.

Now, drawing on this experience, I say, "Yes, but if the generator or external power can keep the batteries charged, that's the same as running them." I frown. "Uh, do we even have a converter?"

"Yes, we do, but it isn't hooked up." Ah, so that's the problem. Jim continues. "When they installed the solar panel they disconnected the converter—and I don't know how to reconnect it." He hesitates. "Well, I could probably reconnect it if I could find the wires—but I don't even know for sure what to look for."

I understand. The converter is located about 15 feet away from any power supply and the no-longer-connected wires hide underneath the chassis who knows where.

And so, I hope Ken can sort the wiring out and make it all work. He agrees to come tomorrow about three.

59. Mixed Up Plans

The next morning, we are out running errands when Jim asks, "Weren't we supposed to be in Vancouver to have lunch with your cousin at two today?"

Oh, yes! Thank goodness, he remembered. Elmer is my brother's age, that is, in his late 80's, but in much poorer health. We usually try to have lunch with him at least once when we are in the area. Elmer and his caregiver friend Leonard go to the same buffet restaurant every weekday for lunch. They are already there when we arrive. In fact, Leonard has his first course and is just sitting down.

Elmer, independent as always, is still picking out his food. He hobbles along the food tables, pushing his walker with his nearly full plate on the seat. He looks up and sees us. Distracted, he stubs his toe on a wheel and the plate goes flying. Fruit gelatin flies out and splats on the floor. Potatoes and gravy fly another direction and just miss the gentleman behind Elmer. The upside-down plate on the floor covers the rest of Elmer's food like a napkin hiding uneaten food. Leonard sits where he is and shakes his head, "He won't let me help him."

Before Jim or I can offer to help, a manager is over talking to Elmer. "That's Dan," Leonard says. "He watches out for us."

Dan signals for a waitress to come clean up the mess on the floor and then turns back to Elmer. "Here, let me help you," he insists. Elmer doesn't argue. My uncle and Dan appear to be old friends. They chat as they move around the food tables filling up another plate, this one held securely in Dan's capable hands. I suspect this is a common occurrence.

Excitement over, Jim and I make our own tour of the food tables. By the time we return with our filled plates, Leonard is has almost finished his first helping. He gets up and brings back a second cup of coffee and a huge dish of ice cream. I remember from previous meals that his first helping is always quite small and as today, he makes up for that with the ice cream. I wonder what he eats at home. Maybe that's when he gets his veggies? He certainly didn't eat many today.

Elmer enjoys talking, but his hearing is bad. Leonard can hear, but talking isn't as easy. Due to a bout with throat cancer years ago, he talks in a loud whisper with lots of extravagant hand motions. I'm concerned that his ice cream dish is going to go flying like Elmer's plate did, but somehow, the flashing hands manage to miss everything on the table.

Elmer sits beside me beaming. He loves to have family visit and there just aren't many of us left anymore. Guess that's the penalty for getting old. You outlive your friends and even much of your family. Elmer has always been tall and slim, and I've never known him with without the beautiful white hair that my father and sisters also had—and I missed. Now, he is shrunken and stooped. His haircut is similar to Jim's—that is, so close it is almost bald. That's where the similarity ends. Jim's still blond hair makes a golden halo around his head. Elmer's pale skin and white hair reminds me of a huge pink tennis ball covered in dandelion fuzz.

We are almost through with our meal when my phone rings. It's Ken, apologizing for being late. Late? Oh, no, we forgot—Ken was coming to come to the yard at 3 o'clock to check Rex's wiring and it's 3:15 now.

"My job is taking longer than I planned. I'll be at least another hour," Ken apologizes.

I breathe a sigh of relief. "That's fine," I tell him without saying we weren't there either. This day isn't going well. I seem to be forgetting things left and right. First Elmer, and now Ken. Is that bump on my head finally taking its toll? Am I developing dementia? Surely not. I simply have too much going on at once—I need to relax and regroup.

However, first we must get back to Rex, hopefully before Ken does. We say goodbye to Elmer and Leonard and dash the 10 miles back to the storage yard. This time, it isn't rush hour and we are home playing cards when Ken shows up at the gate, just like we'd been there the whole time. It reminds me of my old cat, Panther. He'd hear my car and come streaking home, flying through his cat door. By the time I parked my car and unlocked the front door, Panther was inside waiting for me. Just like he'd been there the whole time.

The two men spend less than an hour checking out the wiring.

Ken shakes his head. "I can't really do much without house power," he tells me. Well, maybe next year he can check again when we are parked in a regular campground . . . .

Then Ken grins. "Hey! What about just using a regular car charger?"

Jim looks at him and nods. "Yes, that should work."

Wow! What a simple fix. To think that we could have been doing this all along.

Jim frowns and bursts my bubble. "Well, it would work when we are plugged in at least. There's no way to plug it into the generator when we're dry camping."

"Can't you figure out a way to attach the charger to the generator?" I know I'm asking for a miracle, but I want the whole kahuna. I want to be able to use the generator to charge the batteries too.

"Well, maybe later," Jim promises. I can see I'll have to settle for what we've got for now. And this winter, Jim will have another project.

We thank Ken profusely and give him a goodbye hug. We probably won't see him again until next year.

60. Hurry Up–and Wait

It's moving day again. We want to leave as early in the day as possible, so we rush around and get Rex ready to move out. Before we go, we make a quick trip to Ken's. They are all gone but we want to check our email one more time—we may not get online again for a couple of days—an eternity for computer addicts like us.

We are gone less than an hour, but in that short time the yard looks transformed. A gigantic dirt-moving operation is in process. A string of dirt trucks fill the yard from the open gate to that huge pile of dirt at the far end of the yard. One by one, the trucks fill up with dirt and leave, quickly replaced with another. Jim manages to maneuver between the rigs and park the Saturn back into its usual spot in front of Rex. However, our hook-up-and leave procedure won't be possible until the trucks are out of the way. Usually, that's simple: pull Rex out, situate Froggy behind him and attach. However, there's no moving Rex until the trucks leave. They have the right-of-way.

From our tall front row seats in Rex, we watch Carl operate an ancient front loader, moving dirt from pile to truck. Loaded, the truck rumbles out of the open gate and disappears. Another pulls up to the dirt pile and Carl begins the slow process all over again. Just when we think we'll be able to get out, a third truck pulls into the yard and stops right in front of Rex, waiting its turn.

We'd planned to return the gate key after using it one last time. Because the gate is wide open, I use some of our down-time to take the key over to the manager's trailer now. Remembering Homer's conversation about "working for tips" and Lisa's about preferring a salary to however Dave was paying them, I add a $20 tip, just for Lisa.

I find Lisa is annoyed and eager to vent. It seems that because Dave wanted the couple to work extra hours this week, they had to miss their 18-month-old daughter's visitation. "And we only get to go once a week." Wow! I didn't even know they had a daughter! Like a typical proud mother, she shows me a photo of her little girl. I sympathize with her about her missed visit and "ooh" and "ahh" appropriately about the photo before I take my leave.

Back at the motorhome, I find I haven't escaped bad moods. Jim is fretting. Then his eyes light up. "I think it will work," he mutters as he moves quickly down the steps of the RV. Huh? He's gone before I can ask *what* will work. I watch as he backs Froggy into the presently empty space where the car carrier used to sit. Then he drives Rex forward into the space where the Saturn was, nudging up as close to the parked dirt truck as he dares. Soon, with a little more judicious jockeying of both vehicles, he has the car parked behind Rex, ready for hookup.

Amazing, that man! When the last truck drives out of the still-open gate, Rex, with Froggy in tow, is right behind.

As we travel, I tell Jim about my visit with Lisa, her daughter and their missed visit. "My guess was right," I brag. "Carl and Lisa are recovering addicts who've lost custody of their child." Actually, I'm still guessing, but they definitely fit the profile of many of my former clients.

"It looks to me like Dave has found a way to get cheap labor," Jim comments.

"Could be," I agree. "But I've known business owners who hire recovering addicts, giving them jobs when no one else would. It could be a little of both. Dave gets cheap labor and the couple gets a new start."

We don't know if Dave is being generous and or taking advantage of them. We don't know if Carl and Lisa have a good thing going, or if they are being naive to think that Dave with ever come through. Likely, we'll never know, for we won't be back. Next year, we aren't planning to store Rex, so staying here won't be an option. It feels like we are walking out in the middle of a movie. Still, like good RVers, we are glad to be back on the road.

A Fried
Connection

61. One Last Crisis

Our trip is almost over. With gas still close to $4.00, we decide to store Rex in the comparatively dry Eastern Oregon climate. We will spend our last few days in the Northwest in RV parks, then put Rex into winter storage and drive the Saturn home—without the red Froggy lights. Since we returned from Alaska, and even before, Rex has been behaving like a gentleman. Therefore, we look forward to a luxurious, calm final week.

It was a vain hope. We are in an RV park near where we will leave Rex for the winter. We've returned late from visiting with my Hermiston relatives. I'm fixing supper, and have a chicken and pasta casserole heating in the microwave. It's been a hot day and I'm in my shorts and enjoying the cool feel of the floor on my bare feet.

Suddenly, we are without power. No microwave. No lights. What the . . . ? This sort of thing isn't supposed to happen in RV parks.

We stumble around in the dark, getting in each other's way in the cramped quarters. Jim steps on my bare feet. I squeal and he steps back, avoiding a fall only because the sofa is in the way. "Well, if you'd wear shoes . . . ," he grumbles as he sits heavily onto the sofa. Jim reaches around and opens the shades behind the sofa so we can look outside. Everyone else's lights are working. Just Rex is dark. What now. Is Rex back to his old tricks?

I turn on Rex's battery-powered lights. They work. Jim checks our fuses; they are fine. He digs out the flashlight he keeps handy for just such emergencies and goes outside to check.

"I found the problem," he announces when he returns. "Come look."

We both troupe back out, following the beam of Jim's flashlight. He shines it on the power pole beside Rex. The socket where we had Rex plugged in looks burned as does the three-pronged plug on the end of our cable. Oh, oh. Something has caused a short—it could be worse; it could have caught on fire. It is night, so the office isn't open. Oh, well, we are experienced dry campers.

In the morning, we show the damaged cord to the park manager. Although we have no way of knowing what happened, or even if it was their fault or Rex's, they take responsibility. They give us a new cord and replace the burned socket. With the new cord in the new socket, Rex works fine, so it doesn't seem that he was hurt. Whew! Would that all problems were this easy to fix! Nevertheless, it gives us a taste of how living in RV park luxury has its crises too.

We stow Rex in his winter home. This storage yard is a far cry from the one in Portland. It's all gravel—I certainly wouldn't want to stay here. However, the same climate that doesn't support Portland's greenery makes Hermiston a dryer, better place for Rex now.

We load up the Saturn with things we don't want to leave in Rex over the winter. The trunk and the back seat are crammed. With a last look at Rex, we drive out and head towards home.

Who knows what the future will bring? Maybe next summer, my dream will really come true and we'll be able to use Rex for more than a summer vacation home. Maybe next summer, Rex will be more travel-worthy, with the stopping problem solved and no new crises. Maybe next summer, gas will be less expensive. Maybe next summer . . . .

62. Epilogue

As this goes to print, we still summer in Rex. I did realize my dream when we spent the summer of 2010 doing shows and selling the first book we wrote about Lewy body dementia. We now have another LBD book out and are working on a third. We still do occasional shows and book signings.

We stay mostly at RV parks now, with just a few dry camping stops where that is more practical. Our favorite boondock is the family farm, in Chewelah, WA, where my daughter, Leanne now lives. We watch wild geese and deer from our windows, pick raspberries galore and visit with family.

We still stay in the beauty shop yard when we are in Everett. Bob is in his 90's and still going strong. Iris broke her leg when she was 86. They told her she'd never walk again. She proved them wrong and is walking without a cane except when the going is rough, when she uses two. "They work better for me than a walker," she insists.

We continue to have issues with the dash air conditioning. We finally got it working last year and then this year, found that the coolant had leaked out during the winter. Apparently, we should have been running it occasionally to keep the seals moist.

We did get the new part for the awning. Then, the next year Jim turned a corner too sharp coming out of the RV storage yard here in Mesa and rammed Rex against a post. We had to replace that whole awning arm and Rex now sports a mended hole near the back window.

As for Rex's transmission problem, Jim's internet research suggests that it was an issue specific to that model. Yes, Jim actually did the research! Whatever it was, it quit. Rex never stopped unexpectedly again after the time he stopped outside Mt Shasta City. Nevertheless, we have had plenty of other adventures to keep us on our toes.

We installed wood flooring except for the bedroom where we left the carpet. Then the water pump leaked. We had to replace it and the bedroom carpet. The toilet leaked (thankfully, clean water) and we had to replace it and the new flooring in the bathroom. I left the shower running with only the "stupid button" off. It overfilled the gray water tank and flowed into the bathroom. We had to replace the bathroom flooring—again—and the flooring in the hall. This time we used indoor/outdoor carpets that come up easily, just in case.

Those are the challenges. We've had lots of fun and enjoyment too. We continue to love playing turtle when visiting family and friends—coming complete with our own home. We've met many interesting people, made some good friends and seen a lot of country.

We head out again this summer. Who knows what will happen!